Creative Development

Ashley Compton, Jane Johnston Lindy Nahmad-Williams and Kathleen Taylor

Supporting Development in the Early Years Foundation Stage

continuum

Continuum International Publishing Group

The Tower Building　　　　80 Maiden Lane
11 York Road　　　　　　　Suite 704
London SE1 7NX　　　　　　New York, NY 10038

www.continuumbooks.com

© Ashley Compton, Jane Johnston, Lindy Nahmad-Williams and Kathleen Taylor 2010

Photographs 1.1, 1.2, 1.3, 3.1, 3.2, 3.3, 3.4 and 4.1 used by kind permission of Paul Hopkins (MMI educational consultancy services, www.mmiweb.org.uk). Photographs 2.1 and 4.3 used by kind permission of Emma Jordan E-Services (www.emmajordan-eservices.co.uk). Photographs 2.2a, 2.2b and 2.3 used by kind permission of Edenthorpe Hall Primary School, Doncaster. Photograph 4.2 used by kind permission of Tracy Gannon, Headteacher, Ripley Infant School.

British Library Cataloguing-in-Publication Data
A catalogue record for this book is available from the British Library.

ISBN:　978-1-4411-6330-1 (hardcover)
　　　　978-1-4411-7222-8 (paperback)

Library of Congress Cataloging-in-Publication Data
Creative development / Ashley Compton ... [et al.].
　　p. cm.
　Includes bibliographical references and index.
　ISBN: 978-1-4411-6330-1 (hardback)
　ISBN: 978-1-4411-7222-8 (pbk.)
　1. Early childhood development. 2. Education, Preschool.
　I. Compton, Ashley. II. Title.

　LB1140.2.C742 2010
　305.231–dc22

　　　　　　　　　　　　　2010002889

Typeset by Newgen Imaging Systems Pvt Ltd, Chennai, India
Printed and bound in Great Britain by the MPG Books Group

Contents

Author Details

The authors of this book are experienced educationalists with expertise in Creative Development in the early years.

Ashley Compton

Ashley Compton is a Senior Lecturer on the BA (Hons) in Primary Education with QTS at Bishop Grosseteste University College Lincoln. Her interests include music, mathematics and creativity. Chronicling the development of her two young children has stimulated Ashley's fascination with the early years. She has taught in schools in Canada and the United Kingdom and has also worked as a maths advisory teacher for Lincolnshire.

Jane Johnston

Jane Johnston, one of the series editors, is a Reader in Education at Bishop Grosseteste University College. She has worked as an early years primary classroom practitioner and in early years and primary education initial training. She has a particular interest in early years scientific development (Emergent Science) and is passionate about supporting early years development through exploration and play. Her many publications reflect this interest and she is the author of many books, articles and chapters on early years and science education, including *Early Explorations in Science* published by the Open University Press and *Early Childhood Studies* published by Pearsons.

Lindy Nahmad-Williams

Lindy Nahmad-Williams, one of the series editors, is a Senior Lecturer in Primary Education with responsibility for coordinating learning in the early years on the BA (Hons) in Primary Education with QTS at Bishop Grosseteste University College Lincoln. Her interests include language development,

English and drama and different contexts for learning. She has taught in primary schools in South Yorkshire, Humberside and North Lincolnshire. She has also worked as a Registered Nursery OfSTED inspector and supported teachers in schools across North Lincolnshire in developing language and literacy provision.

Kathleen Taylor

Kathleen Taylor has recently retired from her post as Head of Department for under-graduate Primary Initial Teacher Training at Bishop Grosseteste University College Lincoln. Her interest in the natural environment as a starting point for art and learning led to her involvement in Initial Teacher Education curricular design as well as national curriculum design. She has worked extensively in international contexts, such as in Macedonia, Bosnia Herzegovina and Northern Pakistan. She continues to work in ITE and writes.

Series Editors' Preface

Chapter Outline

Introduction to the series

Before the 10 year strategy (DfES, 2004) and the Childcare Act of 2006, provision for children under 5 years of age was encompassed in a variety of guidance, support and legislation; *Curriculum Guidance for the Foundation Stage* (QCA, 2000), the *Birth to Three Matters* framework (Surestart, 2003), and the *National Standards for Under 8s Daycare and Childminding* (DfES, 2003). This was confusing for many professionals working with young children. The introduction of Early Years Foundation Stage (DCSF, 2008), brought together the main features of each and has provided a structure for the provision of care and education for children from birth to 5 years of age. More importantly it recognized the good practice that existed in each sector of provision and gives a framework or support for further development.

Learning in the Early Years Foundation Stage

The four themes that embody the principles of the Early Years Foundation Stage (EYFS), (DCSF, 2008) succinctly embody the important features of early years provision.

A Unique Child, identifies the importance of child centred provision, recognizing the rapid development in young children and that each child is capable of significant achievements during these years. It is important not to underestimate young children, who may be capable of action, thinking beyond our expectations. It is easy to think that children are too young or not experienced enough to engage in some ideas or activities, but we need to be open-minded as children are very good at exceeding our expectations. Some children may have particular talents, whilst others may be 'all-rounders'. Some children may have particular needs or disabilities. Each child is unique and it is our challenge to ensure that we meet their particular needs, supporting them and challenging them in their development.

Positive Relationships are essential whilst we support and challenge children so that they move from dependence to independence, familiarity to unfamiliarity, learning how to be secure and confident individuals who begin to understand themselves and others. Positive relationships are key to all areas of children's development. Emotional development requires children to have attachments and positive relationships, initially with close family members, but increasingly with secondary carers, peers and other adults. The link between emotional and social development is very strong and positive relationships will also help children to become independent and develop new relationships and begin to see their position and role in society. Positive relationships also support language development, understandings about the world, a range of skills and indeed play a part in all development.

The context in which children develop play a vital part in supporting them in all areas of development. These contexts need to be **Enabling Environments**, or environments that are secure and make children feel confident, that stimulate and motivate children and which support and extend their development and learning. The environment is made up of the physical and the atmospheric. Both need to be warm and secure, so that children feel safe and comfortable and both need to be motivating to encourage children to explore and learn. The environmental atmosphere is also created by the social interactions of all concerned, providing the security that enables a child to move away from the familiar and explore the unfamiliar in a secure and safe way. Indoor environments should provide opportunities for social interaction, language development and creative activities. Outdoor environments may encourage children to develop physically and an interest in the world around them and with opportunities to explore the familiar and unfamiliar world.

Learning and Development indicates the importance of individual children's unique development and learning. As every child is unique, so they have different learning and development needs and will develop in different ways and at different rates. It is important not to assume that all children develop at the same rate. We know that some children begin to walk or talk at a very early age, whilst others take longer, but this does not indicate what they are capable of achieving later in life. Provision for all children needs to be differentiated. In the early years, this is best done by open-ended activities and differentiated interaction and support. Open-ended activities allow children to use and develop from previous experiences and to differentiate for themselves. Support through modelling, questioning and direction can come from experienced peers and adults and will enable the individual child to develop at a rate appropriate for them.

Working within the Early Years Foundation Stage is not without it challenges. Whilst the principles recognize the individual nature of children and their needs, providing this is a different matter. The Early Years Foundation Stage encompasses children in two traditionally distinct phases of development; from birth to 3 years of age and from 3 to 5 years of age. It involves the integration of three overlapping, but traditionally distinct areas of care; social, health and education. Children will have different needs at different ages and in different areas and stages within the EYFS and the challenge is for professionals to meet these diverse needs. It maybe that the norm for children at each age and stage is quite wide and that as many children fall outside of the norm as within it. Care is needed by professionals to ensure that they do not assume that each child is 'normal'.

In order to effectively support children's development in the Early Years Foundation Stage professionals need to have an understanding of child development and share knowledge and understanding in their area of expertise with others whose expertise may lie elsewhere. Professionals from different areas of children's care and provision should work together and learn from each other. Social care, health, educational professionals can all learn from an integrated approach and provide more effective provision as a result. Even within one discipline, professionals can support each other to provide more effective support. Teachers, teaching assistants, special needs coordinators and speech therapists who work in an integrated way can provide better support for individuals. Paediatricians, paediatric nurses, physiotherapist, opticians etc., can support the health care and physical development of children in a holistic way. Early years professionals, behaviour therapists and child psychologists can support the social and emotional development of children. This notion of partnership or teamwork is an important part of integrated working, so that the different types of professionals who work with young children value and respect each other, share knowledge and understanding and always consider the reason for integration; the individual child, who should be at the heart of all we do. Good integrated working does not value one aspect of development above all others or one age of children more than another. It involves different professionals, from early career to those in leadership roles, balancing the different areas of development (health, social, emotional and educational) and ages, ensuring that the key principles of good early years practice are maintained and developed through appropriate interpretation and implementation of the Early Years Foundation Stage.

Another challenge in the Early Years Foundation Stage is to consider the child's holistic progression from birth, through the EYFS to Key Stage 1 and beyond. Working with children in the Early Years Foundation Stage is like being asked to write the next chapter of a book; in order to do this effectively, you need to read the earlier chapters of the book, get to know the main characters and the peripheral characters, understand the plot and where the story is going. However, all the time you are writing you need to be aware that you will not complete the book and that someone else will write the next chapter. If professionals know about individual children, their families, home lives, health and social needs, they will understand problems, issues, developmental needs and be better placed to support the child. If they know where are child will go next, about the differences between the provision in the EYFS and KS1 and even KS2 (remembering the international definition of early childhood is birth to 8 years of age), they can help the child to overcome the difficulties of transition. Transitions occur in all areas of life and at all ages. When we start new jobs, move house, get married, meet new people, go to university, the transition takes some adjustment and involves considerable social and emotional turmoil, even when things go smoothly. As adults we enter these transitions with some knowledge and with a degree of choice, but young children are not as knowledgeable about the transitions that they experience and have less choice in the decisions made about transitions. Babies will not understand that their mother will return soon, small children will not understand that the friends that they made at playgroup are not attending the same nursery or that the routines they have been used to at home and at playgroup have all changed now that they have gone to nursery or started in the foundation unit at school. Professionals working with children, as they move though the many transitions they experience in the first 5 years, need to smooth the pathway for children to ensure that they have smooth and not difficult transitions.

An example of holistic thematic play

Whilst sitting outside a café by the sea in the north of England, the following play was observed. It involved four children representing the whole of early years from about 2 years of age to about 8 years of age; one was about 2 years of age, another about 3 years of age, one about 5 years of age and the fourth about 7 or 8 years of age. The two older children climbed on top of a large wooden seal sculpture and started to imagine that they were riding on top of a swimming seal in the sea. They were soon joined by the 3-year-old child who sat at the foot of the sculpture. 'Don't sit there' said the eldest, 'You are in the sea, you will drown. Climb on the tail, out of the sea'. The two older children helped the 3 year old to climb onto the tail and she and the 5 year old started to slide down the tail and climb up again. Then the children began to imagine that the cars parked nearby were 'whales' and the dogs out with their owners were 'sharks' and as they slid down the tail they squealed that they should 'mind the sharks, they will eat you'. The 5 year old asked what the people sitting outside the café were and the 8 year old said 'I think they can be fishes swimming in the sea'. 'What about the chairs and tables?' asked the 3 year old, to which the older children replied that, 'they can be fishes too'.

At this point, the 2 year old came up to the children and tried to climb up the seal. The three children welcomed her, helped her climb up onto the tail and join them and asked her what her name was. They continued to play and then the mother of the eldest child came to see if the 2 year old was ok and not being squashed in the sliding down the tail. The children did not welcome the interference of an adult and asked her to go away, because 'we are playing, we are playing'. The mother helped the 2 year old to climb down off the seal and the child started to 'swim' on the floor back towards the seal and the other children. The mother said, 'Oh you are getting dirty, get up', but the child kept on 'swimming'. 'Are you being a dog' said the mother 'don't crawl', but the child shook her head and carried on 'swimming' towards the seal, avoiding the fish and sharks!

In this play episode, the children were engaged in holistic play involving aspects of

- Personal, Social and Emotional Development (cooperation);
- Language, Literacy and Communication (communicating with each other and with adults);
- Knowledge and Understanding of the World (applying ideas about animals that live in the sea);
- Creative Development (imaginative play, involving both ludic or fantasy play and epistemic play, or play involving their knowledge).

The adult intervention was, in this case, unhelpful and did not aid the play and illustrates the importance of adults standing back and watching before they interact or intervene.

Supporting development in the Early Years Foundation Stage

This book series consists of six books, one focusing on each of the key areas of the Early Years Foundation Stage and with each book having a chapter for each of the strands that make up that key area of learning. The chapter authors have between them a wealth of expertise in early years provision, as practitioners, educators, policy-makers and authors and are thus well placed to give a comprehensive overview of the sector.

The series aims to look at each of the key areas of the EYFS and support professionals in meeting challenges of implementation and effectively supporting children in their early development. The aim is to do this by helping readers, whether they are trainee, early career or lead professionals:

- to develop deeper understanding of the Early Years Foundation Stage,
- to develop pedagogical skills and professional reflectiveness,
- to develop their personal and professional practice.

Although the series uses the sub-divisions of the key areas of learning and strands within each key area, the authors strongly believe that all areas of learning and development are equally important and inter-connected and that development and learning for children in the early years and beyond is more effective when it is holistic and cross curricular. Throughout the series, links are made between one key area and another and in the introduction to each book specific cross curricular themes and issues are explored. We recognize that language development is a key element in social and emotional development, as well as development in mathematics and knowledge and understanding of the world. We also recognize that the development of attitudes such as curiosity and social skills are key to development in all areas, recognizing the part that motivation and social construction play in learning. In addition, the books use the concept of creativity in its widest sense in all key areas of development and learning and promote play as a key way in which children learn.

Although we believe it is essential that children's learning be viewed holistically, there is also a need for professionals to have a good knowledge of each area of learning and a clear understanding of the development of concepts within each area. It is hoped that each book will provide the professional with appropriate knowledge about the learning area which will then support teaching and learning. For example, if professionals have an understanding of children's developing understanding of cardinal numbers, ordinal numbers, subitizing and numerosity in problem solving, reasoning and numeracy then they will be better equipped to support children's learning with developmentally appropriate activities. Although many professionals have a good understanding of high quality early years practice, their knowledge of specific areas of learning may vary. We all have areas of the curriculum that we particularly enjoy or feel confident in and equally there are areas where we feel we need more support and guidance. This is why each book has been written by specialists in each area of learning, to provide the reader with appropriate knowledge about the subject area itself and suggestions for activities that will support and promote children's learning.

Within each chapter, there is an introduction to the key area, with consideration of the development of children in that key area from birth to 3 years of age; 3 to 5 years of age; into Key Stage 1 (5 to 7 years of age). In this way we consider the holistic development of children, the impact of that development on the key area and the transition from one stage of learning to another in a progressive and 'bottom-up' way. Chapters also contain research evidence and discussions of and reflections on the implications of that research on practice and provision. Boxed features in each chapter contain practical examples of good practice in the key area, together with discussions and reflective tasks for early career professionals and early years leaders/managers, which are designed to help professionals at different stages in their career to continue to develop their professional expertise.

Jane Johnston and Lindy Nahmad-Williams

Books in the series

Broadhead, P., Johnston, J., Tobbell, C. & Woolley, R. (2010) *Personal, Social and Emotional Development*. London: Continuum

Callander, N. & Nahmad-Williams, L. (2010) *Communication, Language and Literacy*. London: Continuum

Beckley, P., Compton, A., Johnston, J. & Marland, H. (2010) *Problem Solving, Reasoning and Numeracy*. London: Continuum

Cooper, L., Johnston, J., Rotchell, E. & Woolley, R. (2010) *Knowledge and Understanding of the World*. London: Continuum

Cooper, L. & Doherty, J., (2010) *Physical Development*. London: Continuum

Compton, A., Johnston, J., Nahmad-Williams, L. & Taylor, K. (2010) *Creative Development*. London: Continuum

References

DCSF (2008) *The Early Years Foundation Stage; Setting the Standard for Learning, Development and Care for Children from Birth to Five; Practice Guidance*. London: DCSF

DfES (2003) *National Standards for Under 8s Daycare and Childminding*. London: DfES

DfES (2004) *Choice for Parents, the Best Start for Children: A Ten Year Strategy for Children*. London: DfES

QCA (2000) *Curriculum Guidance for the Foundation Stage*. London: DFEE

Surestart, (2003) *Birth to Three Matters*. London: DfES

Introduction to Creative Development

Creative development

Many people would think creative development is related to the arts, and the aspects within the EYFS (DCSF, 2008) would appear to confirm this. It is important, however, to read the EYFS introduction to this area of development (DCSF, 2008: 104) to understand that creativity is a far broader concept, which includes risk-taking, making connections, making choices and children initiating learning through exploration. Duffy (1998) also includes problem solving and making connections that lead to new meanings. Craft (2002) makes a clear distinction between imagining and being imaginative, with the latter being a creative process that involves expanding on previous experiences to create something new.

Play and creativity are intrinsically linked. Children use their imagination during play. They make choices, initiate learning, take risks and make connections. It is important that professionals recognize the potential of play and provide space, time and resources that can be used in a variety of ways to encourage children to use their imagination to create their own play situations. Broadhead et al. (2010), in the *Personal, Social and Emotional Development* title in this book series, discusses the play area called 'Whatever you want to be place' which has resources such as boxes, material, clothes, horses, etc. to encourage open-ended possibilities in play. Providing children with opportunities to make music, to move freely and to explore a range of media gives them the opportunity to express themselves and develop their own ideas. There is a move towards a more creative curriculum in primary education in response to the Independent Review of the Primary Curriculum (Rose, 2009) and this is also a key theme within the Cambridge Review (Alexander, 2009). Young children's natural curiosity, drive to explore and immersion in play are the foundations of creativity. As professionals, we must nurture, not stifle, this natural creative instinct to enable young children to develop into the innovative, creative thinkers of the future.

Holistic development in creative development

The outdoor area in a nursery had a number of different resources and uses of space to encourage creativity.

Sharma and Darcy were dancing round the area waving chiffon scarves that they had found in the dressing-up box. Sharma put one over her head and said she had long hair. Darcy tried to tie hers around her waist. It kept falling off until she realized she could tuck it into the waistband of her trousers. Sharma then grabbed the back of it and told her horse to 'giddyup'. Darcy became the horse, trotting and bowing her head up and down with Sharma following behind with the scarf around her head.

Kaylee was drawing a line on the ground with chalk around the outdoor area. She very carefully wrote a 'K' at the beginning and then drew round the edge of the outdoor area going round the water tray and sand area. When a child started to walk on the line she had drawn, Kaylee said, 'This is my map. I'm drawing a map so people know where to go. Follow my map'.

Alfie and Jack were running on the grassed area playing tigers. They were running, growling and throwing themselves on top of each other. Amy and Ki joined them as hunters, chasing them and firing shots from their imaginary rifles. Amy shouted she had got one, Ki said he had got two, Amy shouted they had to catch three more and the children carried on running, interchanging between being tigers and hunters.

Large pieces of paper had been taped to the fence. Adam and Josie were using decorator paintbrushes and were making a rainbow with large paint strokes. Adam began to add large, blue splodges which he said was the rain. Josie said rain was brown and began to add brown splodges. Adam said it was mud from the tractor and began to paint a brown tractor, talking about working on the farm. Nearby, Tiffany was making circular shapes with shells and pebbles on the ground. She then began to alternate between a pebble and a shell to make the circle. She was very particular about which pebble or shell she selected, often rejecting those she wasn't happy with.

It is clear that the children in the above scenarios were playing and using their imagination and were exploring media and materials. The other areas of learning are also evident:

- Personal, Social and Emotional Development – making relationships, making choices, working together, concentrating, demonstrating confidence and independence;
- Communication, Language and Literacy – communicating successfully with one another both verbally and non-verbally, creating a narrative through painting and imaginative play, writing initial letters;
- Problem solving, Reasoning and Numeracy – counting, understanding 'more', making shapes, creating repeating patterns;
- Knowledge and Understanding of the World – understanding places and the purpose of maps, exploring natural materials, knowledge of different environments (in the wild, on the farm) and different animals;
- Physical Development – running, jumping, trotting, falling safely, spatial awareness, fine motor control.

Structure of this book

In Chapter 1, Being Creative, Jane Johnston outlines what being creative means by discussing seminal research in this complex area of learning. Rather than attempting to define creativity in narrow terms, Jane offers the reader ways of thinking about creativity that will help to support children's development. In Chapter 2, Exploring Media and Materials, Kathleen Taylor focuses specifically on painting, drawing, clay and printing to support professionals in understanding the skills needed to work with these mediums and knowledge of how to support children's development through provision of materials and sensitive interactions. In Chapter 3, Creating Music and Dance, Ashley Compton provides a comprehensive overview of the key features of music and dance and considers a range of issues including composing, performing, resourcing and progression. In Chapter 4, Developing Imagination and Imaginative Play, Jane Johnston and Lindy Nahmad-Williams discuss different approaches to play and ways to promote children's use of imagination. Different approaches to teaching drama in the early years are also considered.

The case studies and reflective tasks will also help professionals to reflect on their own practice, consider the theories and research underpinning effective practice and enable them to identify how they can (and why they should) develop their practice. These case studies are designed at two levels; the early career professional and the early-years leader. The early-years professional may be a student/trainee who is developing their expertise in working with young children and, for them, the reflective tasks encourage them to look at the case studies and engage in some critical thinking on issues that are pertinent for early-years education. They will also be able to use the chapters to develop their understanding of issues in knowledge and understanding of the world and try out some of the ideas to develop their skills supporting children in this important area of development. The reflective tasks for early career professionals are also relevant to professionals who are in the early part of their career and to help them not only in their day-to-day interactions with children but also to help them to be engaged in the national debates about good practice and educational theories. The second level of reflective tasks are geared towards the early-years leader, who has a strategic role to develop the practice of those who work with them and also the children in the early-years setting. They would be interested on the impact on both the adult professional development and raising standards in knowledge and understanding of the world in young children in their setting. The reflective tasks may well be ones that can be addressed as part of a staff meeting or staff development session and can follow the practical tasks so that professionals at all levels can share ideas and experiences, identify factors affecting their support for children, both positive factors and challenges to overcome. In this way professionals can discuss their own and other's practice, share successes, support each other and come to realize that there is not one model of good practice, one recipe, that if we all follow will automatically lead to success in children's development and help the setting achieve outstanding recognition in inspections.

We hope that professionals reading this book both enjoy and find the content useful in their professional lives.

References

Alexander, R. (ed.) (2009) *Children, their World, their Education: Final Report and Recommendations of the Cambridge Review.* London: Routledge

Broadhead, P., Johnston, J., Tobbell, C. and Woolley, R. (2010) *Personal, Social and Emotional Development.* London: Continuum

Craft, A. (2002) *Creativity and Early Years Education.* London: Continuum

DCSF (2008) *The Early Years Foundation Stage; Setting the Standard for Learning, Development and Care for Children from Birth to Five; Practice Guidance.* London: DCSF

Duffy, B. (1998) *Supporting Creativity and Imagination in the Early Years.* Buckingham: Open University Press

Rose, J. (2009) *The Independent Review of the Primary Curriculum Final Report.* Nottingham: DCSF

1 Being Creative

Introduction

Being creative involves bringing something new into being, particularly something that has value to someone. This can be a painting, dance, film, idea, invention, new car etc., although what one person values, another person may not and so not consider it as creativity. This is well exampled by the media controversy that accompanies some conceptual art, such as Tracey Emin's bed (Emin, 1998) or Damien Hirst's cow and calf in tanks (Hirst, 2007). In the same way children can create something that is not valued at all or only by their family, friends or carers. This may be a mess which is unlikely to be valued by carers; pictures and models, which their parents value and pin on walls and fridge doors; profound statements or original and significant comments which are stored away to retell as they grow up or recount to friends. I remember my sister making a scarf for my father which was full of holes from dropped stitches and curiously got thin in the middle and then thickened out.

My father would put it on each morning, leave the house and walk to the end of the road, before taking it off and putting it in his pocket, putting it on again as he approached the house at the end of the day. As a teacher, children would give you cakes they had made, adorned with thick coloured icing, and sprinkles of the edible and non-edible, which I would 'save' to eat later!

Being creative is a complex concept, which many researchers, writers (e.g. de Bono, 1992; Beetlestone, 1998; Craft, 2000) and policy makers (e.g. NACCCE, 1999; DfES, 2003; QCA, 2003; Roberts, 2006) have attempted to define, with no clear agreement (Gibson, 2005). Being creative can involve lateral thinking and problem solving (de Bono, 1992), as well as discovery (DES, 1967; Johnston, 2004) and imagination (Craft, 2000) and is not exclusive to the arts (Prentice, 2000; Wilson, 2009). Beetlestone (1998) identified six categories in defining creativity. The first category is creativity as a form of learning, or creativity in everyday life; little c (Craft, 2002). This involves creativity as being curious, encouraging children in exploration, investigation and invention in order to understand abstract concepts, as explored in the companion books in this series; *Knowledge and Understanding of the World* (Cooper et al., 2010), *Communication, Language and Literacy* (Callendar and Nahmad-Williams, 2010) and *Problem Solving, Reasoning and Numeracy* (Beckley, 2010). Beetlestone's (1998) second category, representation involves the more traditional idea of using media to express ideas and feelings. This can be through art, drama, music and play (see Policastro and Gardner, 1999) and as explored in other chapters of this book. The third category, productivity (Beetlestone, 1998) also follows the more traditional definition of making something new and also involves destroying the old, while the fourth category, originality, moves and extends the definition by including making connections, possibly in a new and novel way; (de Bono, 1992; Duffy, 1998) and taking risks. Creative thinking (de Bono, 1992) and problem solving (Policastro and Gardner, 1999; Johnston, 2009), the fifth category (Beetlestone, 1998), involves the application of knowledge and skills, maybe learnt from past experiences, in new contexts. This application of ideas involves analyzing and synthesizing ideas (Gardner, 2007) and recognizing patterns and analogies. Beetlestone's (1998) final category is universe/creation-nature and involves a personal and emotional response to the world and can be seen in the awe and wonder observed in children when they a faced with a new experience or see an old experience in a different way.

Being creative is therefore something that is present in all children and not limited to gifted and talented children. It is an attribute that can be developed and encouraged but not really taught. Being creative is one of the five minds (or ways of processing) identified by Howard Gardner (2007) and which he feels will be of increasing importance in our future lives. The 5 minds are,

1 The Disciplined Mind: developed through education and supports individuals in becoming 'expert' in one discipline.
2 The Synthesizing Mind: involving the skills of synthesis or the ability to survey a wide range of sources or experiences, make decisions about their importance, combine information in a meaningful way and communicate that in an understandable way.
3 The Creating Mind.
4 The Respectful Mind: which involves welcoming social contact, displaying initial trust, giving individuals the benefit of the doubt, trying to form links, being tolerant and avoiding making judgements.
5 The Ethical Mind: which considers more sophisticated moral issues in an abstract way.

Synesthesia is a neurologically based phenomenon which can be seen in children, where senses are linked and stimulation of one sensory or cognitive pathway leads a response in another. Many creative people are known or thought to be synesthetes; the Finnish composer Jean Sibelius and the Hungarian composer Franz Liszt saw sounds as colours, as does the artist David Hockney, while the Russian writer Vladimir Nabokov associated graphemes with colour. It is thought, but not proven, that babies have these links, but as they develop the connections get broken in most cases. Where they do not, the child becomes a synesthete and has the propensity for a greater creative response to stimuli. Girls also are able to see more colours than boys as they have two X chromosomes, containing the genes for colour vision. However, there is no evidence that girls have a greater creative response to colour as compared to boys.

The creating mind is a restless one, constantly developing new ideas, practices and procedures, solving complex problems and being innovative (see also Csikszentmihalyi, 1997). The creative individual will not risk failure and is motivated to continually create. The minds are interrelated in a mutually supportive way. Being creative alone is not enough as without a disciplined and synthesizing mind creativity will not be focused or have an impact. A disciplined mind is needed to be able to synthesize and be creative and creativity involves some degree of synthesis, although a very disciplined mind is less likely to be creative and a highly synthesizing mind may not lead to creativity.

Policy recognition for being creative

The Early Years Foundation Stage (DCSF, 2008) recognizes the wide definition of being creative as described above. They identify creativity as being about more than art, craft, dance and imagination. It is about children taking risks, making connections, becoming absorbed in their work, that is, play. However, this recognition has been hard won. The *All our Futures* (NACCCE, 1999) took a wide view of creativity, believing that everyone is capable of, and have a democratic right, to be creative and to be a function of education. They also recognized that creative teaching was an essential contributing factor for creative learning. This has not always been evident in policy and support documents, with proscribed teaching approaches (e.g. DfEE, 1998; DfEE, 1999) in compulsory education that have had a detrimental affect on early-years provision. Indeed, *All our Futures* (NACCCE, 1999) had a limited impact as it was not widely publicized or circulated. The Primary strategy (DfES, 2003), support documents (QCA, 2003) and more recent reports (Roberts, 2006) have emphasized the importance of creativity in learning at an early age. The key issues from the Roberts (2006: 8) report recognize the work on developing creativity in the early years, but identify that creativity is not fully supported by the 'many creative programmes, projects and agencies'. They also recommend stronger connections between practice and policy, but the emphasis on a 'secure, valued and cost-effective framework for the further development of creativity, both its own right and as a support for economic growth, with better outcomes for children and young people', leaves me with some concern about their definition of creativity and the use of that definition. This is reinforced by the practical recommendations which focus on policy rather than practice and leave much to interpretation and the creative mind!

1 Ensure the visibility of creativity in the Early Learning goals and in the guidance for Children's Centres.

2 Establish a best practice recognition scheme for creativity in Early-Years settings with associated workforce development for education and creative practitioners.

3 Establish parental/family support programmes with creative parent/child learning. (Roberts, 2006: 9)

Being creative from birth to 3 years of age

From the moment of conception a baby responds to its environment. In the womb, the developing foetus will respond to sounds, waving arms and kicking legs and will feel pleasure and pain. When they are born, babies recognize sounds and experiences, which have given them pleasure and make links between their movement and senses. They respond to sensory input; what they see, hear, smell, touch and feel and will show a response by smiling, making noises or moving their limbs. Rhymes, songs and stories will elicit responses which in themselves are unique and creative. Children will respond by repeating sounds, actions and attempt to make sense of what they are experiencing. In this way they are making connections between different experiences and sensations. More detail of specific developments can be read in the other chapters of this book, Chapter 2: Exploring Media and Materials, Chapter 3: Creating Music and Dance and Chapter 4: Developing Imagination and Imaginative Play and also in other books in this series. For example, a child responding to a number rhyme will be developing understanding of numbers, language, rhythm and rhyme. They may also make movements in response to the rhyme and create a patterned response in a form of dance.

Case study

Simon and Sean are 1-year-old identical twins but their response to experiences is not always the same. When their mother sings to them, Simon loves to hear,

> Ring a Ring of Roses,
> A pocket full of poses,
> A-tishoo! A-tishoo!
> We all fall Down.

On hearing the rhyme, Simon bounces up and down, holds his hands out to others and drops to the floor at the end. Sean smiles and sings *A-tishoo! A-tishoo!*

Sean prefers to hear the rhyme,

> Horsey horsey don't you stop
> Just let your feet go clippetty clop
> The tail goes swish and the wheels go round
> Giddy up, we're homeward bound.

He repeats the sounds *clippetty clop* and *swish* at the appropriate places. Simon responds to this rhyme by bouncing up and down in a rhythmical way.

Reflection for the early career professional

- How are Simon and Sean's responses to the rhymes different but creative responses?
- Why might different children make different creative responses to stimuli or experiences?

Reflection for the leader/manager

- How does your setting encourage different responses?
- Are there any ways in which you can encourage and accommodate differing responses to experiences and stimuli?

An important part of being creative, involves risk taking and problem solving. This can involve children *being different* and this is sometimes easier for children in the youngest age group, but gets increasingly harder as they begin to socialize and learn that there are norms, which being different from are not always acceptable. Young boys who like to dress up in a range of make-up and female roles may be discouraged by other boys or even by parents who worry about them being 'sissy' or that their sexuality may be affected. Girls who like to play football or play with construction toys may also be discouraged by peers or adults. Risk taking in young children may involve something familiar to the adult professional, but it is new and novel and risky for the child (Clare and Woolley, 2009). Children should be encouraged to take risks; that is, not to be unsafe but to risk doing or being different in actions and responses. Professionals working with children need to be open to different responses and consider that just because a response is different, it is not wrong. Educationalists tend not to be highly creative (Johnston, 1996) and this can constrain children in their responses and limit their creativity.

Being creative from 3 to 5 years of age

As children develop they are increasingly less likely to take risks, as they conform to the rules of the setting and do not wish to be different. This can be discussed through circle-time activities (see Mosely, 2009) or through the use of puppets, so that children can express themselves in a safe environment, where they can take risks (Beetlestone, 1998) and be different through the puppet. There is some research evidence for the use of puppets in helping children to communicate ideas in science education (Naylor et al., 2007), but some anecdotal evidence for the effectiveness of other techniques to support creative communication. As children develop, they are also able to communicate their responses with others, moving from communicating with close adults to peers. They will join in and repeat songs and rhymes. They will articulate which are their favourite songs and why. They will show others the things they have made (paintings, sticking, threading), roles they have created by dressing up or music they have composed and explain how they made them. Some children may get frustrated with the creative process or be unhappy with their creations if they have high expectations and expect the finished product to look or sound like a professional product. What is important is to harness this frustration so that it becomes a motivation to continue to create, rather than persuade them that they cannot be creative. They will continue to develop and share their personal preferences, as in the case study above and may spend long periods of time engaged in some creative activities. In one exploration of different materials in a nursery class, João became fascinated by the finger painting and spent the whole session creating different patterns in the paint and on paper with the paint. Andrea did not like the feel of the paint on her fingers and so chose not to finger paint, but she explored the use of colour wash on paper, using a large brush. The children were encouraged to talk about their different preferences and other children were also able to share their preferences.

As children develop physically and emotionally, they will be able to show a range of responses to music, media and phenomena. They will express their preferences in different ways, so that a feeling of sadness or joy can be expressed through painting, imaginative role-play, creating music and in modelling. They will not only develop preferences for forms of expression, but be able to discuss these and compare the creative products produced using a different media, evaluating the results. They will also be able to use a variety of tools to help with their creations. We must be careful not to underestimate the ability of children of this age, as they are capable of producing high quality creative products. A visit to an historic house will show evidence of children under 5 years of age making samplers, producing quality water-coloured paintings, writing stories and plays. Whether they were able to express and communicate their creative ideas, or make decisions for themselves about how to approach their creative products is unclear.

Case study

Children in a nursery setting had been on a visit to a wildlife park and afterwards the professional brought in books, pictures and toys of monkeys and apes. After a circle time where they looked at the differences between monkeys and apes the children then went on to paint pictures of them. Sonia painted a really good picture of some monkeys. There were three of them in a tree in different positions. They were in different positions in the tree, sitting, climbing and swinging. It was very clear what they were and there was a sense of both the relationships and movement. It was Sonia's own idea, not copied but developed from the discussion about the things monkeys did. The professional talked with Sonia about her picture and praised her for the quality of the ideas and the skill of execution. Later, while the professional was talking with some of the other children, she noticed Sonia was continuing to paint. She continued her painting until her monkey picture was completely obscured with a coating of browny-black paint.

Reflection for the early career professional

- How would you have responded to Sonia's continuation of her painting?
- Would different responses be appropriate? Explain why or why not.

⇨

Case study—Cont'd

- How could you encourage Sonia to articulate her ideas about the process and product of creation?

Reflection for the leader/manager

- Use the case study with your staff to consider whether the focus in the early years should be on the process of creation or the value of the product? Provide a rationale for your decisions.
- How could you create opportunities for children to discuss both the process and the product of creation?

Photograph 1.1 Child painting (© P. Hopkins)

Transition to Key Stage 1 (5 to 7 years of age)

By the time children enter formal education at Key Stage 1, they will be more able to communicate their ideas, feelings and choices and listen to those of others, but they will probably be less willing to take risks or be different, as they may have learnt that this can cause problems.

Case study

Six children were playing with a collection of toys on a table in a Reception/Year 1 class. Sam was a Reception child aged 4 1/2 years who had only recently started in the class. Most experiences were new to Sam and he would normally play with toys on the floor and not sit around a table. As the children were playing, Sam's toy fell on the floor and he was unsure whether he should move from the table to collect it, but he wanted to play with it and so with his bottom firmly in his seat, he tried to reach the toy with his foot. Sam had quickly learnt a rule in the classroom; when sitting at a table, you do not wander round the room!

Reflection for the early career professional

- How would you respond to Sam?
- How could you promote a discussion with the children about different responses to situations?

Reflection for the leader/manager

- How can you find out how children view the rules and norms of your setting?
- How can you encourage 'safe' but different and creative responses in children?
- How can you encourage children to respond in different and creative ways?

At Key Stage 1, many creative responses can be embedded in subjects. In mathematics, children can discuss different ways to solve a number problem, or applying ideas from one subject to another, or communicate their reasoning in solving a problem in a variety of ways; practically, oral, pictorially. In science, they may discuss their findings, use puppets to articulate their ideas (see Naylor et al., 2007), or even engage in drama of drawn cartoons to show what they have found out. In history, hot seating can help children to communicate and share ideas about the intentions and emotions of historical figures or surrounding historical events (see Johnston et al. 2007). They may use language in a creative way, making up new words to describe their experiences and emotions. They should be able to see patterns in the results of explorations and investigations in a variety of subjects (mathematics, geography, technology and science), develop simple theories and apply these in different contexts, explaining the reason for decisions and responses to both peers and adults.

Photograph 1.2 Science investigation (© P. Hopkins)

How can we support creativity?

Creative children can be identified by their ability to make connections and see patterns and relationships. They may be challenging and questioning, imaginative and inventive. They will be able to explore ideas, not to make decisions and reflect critically on what they have done and achieved. Being creative is fundamental to successful learning in all areas. Creative children need creative teachers who make connections between aspects of learning across the curriculum (Duffy, 1998). This is increasingly recognized at all stages of the early years and primary curriculum (DfES, 2003; DCSF, 2008; Rose, 2009). A creative professional would have the knowledge and understanding of the key areas to be developed and have good pedagogy skills. They would be confident in the creative approaches to development and learning, being able to extend or adapt ideas rather than follow a recipe approach, producing novel ideas for achieving objectives. They would also be enthusiastic learners and teachers and would balance the needs of the curriculum with those of the individual's creative development, balancing creativity and knowledge (Boden, 2001). A creative teacher therefore demonstrates commitment, subject knowledge, pedagogical knowledge and involvement with the task. They also demonstrate an ability to give guidance, or give direction and focus, be both sensitive and aware, listen actively, protect pupils against disparagement and ridicule, recognize when real effort needs further encouragement and foster a climate which supports creative ideas.

Creative environments

Creative environments are an essential support for creative development. The Early Years Foundation Stage (DCSF, 2008) identify the importance of positive relationships, so that children feel secure enough to be adventurous and take risks and where their creative responses are valued and not considered wrong (Treffinger, 1984), even if they are nonconformist. It is interesting to note that socialization brings with it greater conformity and less creativity. For example, the percentage of original responses can be ascertained through ideational fluency tasks; where potential creativity is assessed through generation of possible uses for a familiar item like a piece of paper. Four-year-old children have been seen (Moran et al., 1983) to have a 50 per cent ideational fluency and this drops to 25 per cent during early schooling, before returning to 50 per cent among college students. This appears to indicate that as children develop, they are not given the opportunity to express divergent thought and to find more than one route to solutions.

Creative adult support

Creative learners require support to encourage creative responses, as 'creativity is not simply a matter of "letting go"' (NACCCE, 1999: 42). Professionals not only need to value what children can do and children's own ideas rather than expecting them to reproduce or imitate (DCSF, 2008) but also to support creative responses. This does not mean that children should be allowed free expression, have no constraints or inhibitions, but rather that adults should provide structures and develop creative techniques that can enhance their natural talents and develop skills that can be applied in a variety of contexts and help to produce valued products. As de Bono (1992) has identified, naturally creative individuals can be more creative with some training and techniques and all individuals can develop their creativity with support. Professionals need to recognize children's creative capacities and provide the particular conditions in which they can be developed, developing cultural knowledge and understanding (see also Clare and Wolley, 2009).

Beetlestone (1998: 6) sees creative support as more than good practice, involving 'a complex interplay between the child, the teacher and the context in such a way that each element is pushing forward, seeking new boundaries, striving towards new territories, always looking to extend in the search of something new'. Roberts (2006) identifies support for creativity in the early years as an essential foundation for lifelong learning and recommends that early years settings encourage creativity behaviours. Teachers are felt (Roberts, 2006) to be able to support creativity by clarity about the purpose of any task and the rules, freedoms and constraints in which they must work. They also should adapt to children's ideas, rather than expecting children to adapt to their ideas (Rousseau, 1911; NACCCE, 1999), being accepting and non-judgmental, welcoming both divergent and convergent thinking and encouraging children to move from familiar and popular ideas to the more original and inventive ones. Professionals can also accommodate differing religious or cultural beliefs particularly where they are represented in different ways and this can encourage cultural understandings and diversity. There is also an emphasis on the process, rather than the product, but as our case study above shows, we do need to value the product too.

If children are given complete freedom to be creative with no adult support, the result is likely to be unplanned chaos, with little regard to the choice of resources, mess, wastage and the learning is likely to be minimal too, if for no other reason than the process and product are not apparent. If the activity is carefully planned and prepared and the adult supports and intervenes at the appropriate time, then children with different creative abilities and potentials can be supported and each process and product is explicitly valued and intrinsic motivation is encouraged. Extrinsic motivation, in the form of rewards or incentives are thought (Groves et al., 1987) to inhibit creativity, reducing the quality of responses and the flexibility of thought in ideational tests and it may be that more creative children are motivated by intrinsic, rather than extrinsic factors.

Creative activities

Creative activities can spark imaginations (Roberts, 2006) and develop thinking skills (Costello, 2000; Shayer and Adey, 2002). Creative activities involve children in working in groups with others and articulating their ideas. The professional can open dialogue with the children asking open-ended questions and encouraging them to question themselves and others. This may include giving children opportunities to work with a variety of creative adults, such as artists, inventors, actors and dancers and to discuss with them the way they express themselves and the different responses to media (DCSF, 2008).

The range of resources used in activities can support creativity. These can include cultural artefacts to support cultural understandings and consideration of cultural responses. Children can use their senses to explore resources and respond to the touch, smell, taste and sounds they experience. Children with sensory impairment will often focus on other senses, rather than the one that is impaired. Children with visual impairment will often put things to their mouths and cheeks to feel them and children with hearing impairments will look closely and touch resources to find out about them. Often children who are able-bodied rely on their sense of sight to the detriment of other senses and it can be good to provide experiences that focus on other senses. It is important to get the children to share what they feel, see, hear with others, so that they realize that not everyone has the same emotional response to particular stimuli.

The creative use of the outdoor environment is also important (Jeffrey and Woods, 2003) as children do have a greater creative response (Johnston, 2005) and show greater observational skills (Johnson and Tunnicliffe, 2002). I will often ask children to explore their local environment using their senses. They close their eyes and focus on their sense of smell or sound or touch. They identify what the world around them feels like by feeling the ground under their feet, the sun on their faces and the girth and feel of the tree trunks. They can listen to the sounds of birds, the wind in the trees or a car passing. They can represent these experiences in a variety of ways through music, paint, modelling etc., and they can discuss the different responses to the same experience and the reasons why they have used this media.

Photograph 1.3 Playing outside (© P. Hopkins)

Other creative activities may involve making a product and this gives children the opportunity to evaluate both the process and the product (Prentice et al., 2003). Much of the evaluation is thought (Sefton-Green, 2000) to be a creative, collective dialogue and, if the environment is one that values children's ideas, then children will feel able to express their ideas about their product and the process of creating it. Remember that a product can be an idea, a problem, as well as a sound, painting etc.

Creative activities require time to be truly effective so that children can explore, develop ideas and finish working on their ideas. In a busy setting, this can be difficult to achieve and some children may need more time than others, spending hours repeating, practicing and perfecting. In many activities, it is easy to forget to give the time for children to complete the creative process and even more difficult to find the time to share, discuss and evaluate.

Practical tasks

Plan an activity for the children in your setting that allows them to be creative in their response. You could use the other chapters of this book to give you ideas about the focus of the activity. Ensure that the activity is open-ended enough to allow for creativity, have time to enable children to produce differentiated responses and to share, discuss and evaluate their responses.

Reflection for the early career professional

- How do Beetlestone's (1998) tiers relate to the activity you have planned?
- How do different children respond to the activity in creative ways?
- How can you modify the activity to provide a greater creative response?

Reflection for the leader/manager

- What are the implications of Beetlestone's (1998) three tiers on your work with young children?
- How can you develop further activities that enable every child to be creative?

References

Beckley, P., Compton, A., Johnston, J. and Marland, H. (2010) *Problem Solving, Reasoning and Numeracy.* London: Continuum

Beetlestone, F. (1998) *Creative Children, Imaginative Teaching.* Buckingham: Open University Press

Boden, M. A. (2001) 'Creativity and Knowledge'. In Craft, A., Jeffrey, B. and Leibling, M. (eds) *Creativity in Education.* London: Continuum

Callander, N and Nahmad-Williams, L. (2010) *Communication, Language and Literacy.* London: Continuum

Clare, H. and Woolley, R. (2009) 'What has Creativity got to do with Citizenship Education'. In Wilson, A. (ed.) *Creativity in Primary Education.* 2nd Edition. Exeter: Learning Matters, 155–171

Costello, P. J. M. (2000) *Thinking Skills and Early Childhood Education.* London: David Fulton

Cooper, L., Johnston, J., Rotchell, E. and Woolley, R. (2010) *Knowledge and Understanding of the World.* London: Continuum

Craft, A. (2000) *Creativity across the Primary Curriculum.* London: Routledge

Craft, A. (2002) *Creativity and Early Years Education; A Lifewide Foundation.* London: Continuum

Csikszentmihalyi, M. (1997) *Creativity.* New York: HarperPerennial

DCSF (2008) *The Early Years Foundation Stage; Setting the Standard for Learning, Development and Care for Children from Birth to Five; Practice Guidance.* London: DCSF

De Bono (1992) *Serious Creativity.* London: Harper Collins

DES (1967) *Children and their Primary school. A Report of the Central Advisory Council for Education (England) Vol. 1: Report.* London: HMSO

DfEE (1998) *The National Literacy Strategy.* London: DFEE

DfEE (1999) *The National Curriculum: Handbook for Teachers in England.* London: DfEE/QCA

DfES (2003) *Excellence and Enjoyment. A strategy for Primary Schools.* London: DfES

Duffy, B. (1998) *Supporting Creativity and Imagination in the Early Years.* Buckingham: Open University Press

Emin, T. (1998) 'My Bed'. www.saatchi-gallery.co.uk/artists/tracey_emin.htm accessed 25/6/09

Gardner, H. (2007) *Five Minds for the Future.* Harvard: Harvard Business School

Gibson, H. (2005) 'What Creativity Isn't: The Presumptions of Instrumental and Individual Justifications for Creativity in Education', *British Journal of Educational Studies,* Vol. 53, No. 2: 148–167

Groves, M. M., Sawyers, J. and Moran, J. III. (1987) 'Reward and Ideational Fluency in Preschool Children'. *Early Childhood Research Quarterly,* Vol. 2: 335–340

Hirst, D. (2007) 'Mother and Child Divided exhibition copy (original 1993)'. www.tate.org.uk/servlet/ViewWork?cgroupid=999999961andworkid=99670&searchid=9402 accessed 25/6/09

Jeffrey, B. and Woods, P. (2003) *The Creative School. A Framework for Success, Qulaity and Effectiveness.* London: RoutledgeFalmer

Johnson, S. and Tunnicliffe, S. D. (2000) 'Primary Children Talk about Plants in the Garden'. Paper Presented to the NARST Conference, April 2000, USA

Johnston C. (1996) *Unlocking the Will to Learn.* California: Corwin Press Inc

Johnston, J. (2004) 'The Value of Exploration and Discovery'. *Primary Science Review,* Vol. 85: 21–23, Nov/Dec 2004

Johnston, J. (2005) *Early Explorations in Science.* 2nd Edition. Maidenhead: Open University Press

Johnston, J. (2009) 'What is Creativity in Science Education'. In Wilson, A. (ed.) *Creativity in Primary Education.* 2nd Edition. Exeter: Learning Matters, 88–101

Johnston, J., Halocha, J. and Chater, M. (2007) *Developing Teaching Skills in the Primary School.* Maidenhead: Open University Press

Johnson, S. and Tunnicliffe, S. D. (2000). Primary children talk about plants in the garden. P*aper presented to the NARST Conference, April 2000, USA.*

Moran, J. D. III, Milgrim, R., Sawyers, J. and Fu, V. (1983) 'Original Thinking in Preschool Children'. *Child Development,* Vol. 54: 921–926

Mosely, J. (2009) 'Jenny Mosely's Quality Circle Time'. www.circle-time.co.uk/ accessed 30/6/09

NACCCE (National Advisory Committee on Creative and Cultural Education) (1999) *All Our Futures: Creativity, Culture and Education.* London: DfEE

Naylor S., Keogh B., Downing, B., Maloney, J. and Simon, S. (2007) 'The Puppets Project: Using Puppets to Promote Engagement and Talk in Science'. In Pinto, R. and Couso, D. (eds) *Contributions from Science Education Research.* Dordrecht: Springer, 289–296

Policastro, E. and Gardner, H. (1999) 'From Case Studies to Robust Generalizations: An Approach to the Study of Creativity'. In Sternberg, R. J. (ed.) *Handbook of Creativity.* Cambridge: Cambridge University Press, 213–225

Prentice, R. (2000) 'Creativity: A Reaffirmation of Its Place in Early Childhood Education'. *The Curriculum Journal*, Vol. 11, No. 2: 145–158

Prentice, R., Matthews, J. and Taylor, H. (2003) 'Creative Development: Learning and the Arts'. In Riley, J. (ed.) *Learning in the Early Years. A guide for Teachers of Children 3–7.* London: Paul Chapman, 185–218

QCA (2003) *Creativity: Find it Promote it.* London: QCA/DFEE

Roberts, P. (2006) *Nurturing Creativity in Young People. A Report to Government to Inform Future Policy.* London: DCMS

Rose, J. (2009) *Independent Review of the Primary Curriculum: Final Report.* Nottingham: DCFS

Rousseau, J. J. (1911) *Emile.* London: J. M. Dent and Sons

Sefton-Green, J. (2000) 'From Creativity to Cultural Production. Shared Perspectives'. In Sefton-Green, J. and Sinker, R. (eds) *Evaluating Creativity. Making and Learning by Young People.* London: Routledge, 216–231

Shayer, M. and Adey, P (eds) (2002) *Learning Intelligence. Cognitive Acceleration Across the Curriculum from 5 to 15 Years.* Buckingham: Open University Press

Treffinger, D. J. (1984) 'Creative Problem-Solving for Teachers'. Lecture delivered to Project Interact Spring Conference, Radford, VA, April

Wilson, A. (ed.) (2009) *Creativity in Primary Education.* 2nd Edition. Exeter: Learning Matters

2 Exploring Media and Materials

Chapter Outline

Introduction

Exploring media and materials is an aspect of Creative Development, one of the six areas of learning and development identified in the Statutory Framework for the Early Years Foundation Stage (EYFS) (DCSF, 2008). It is particularly associated with the art and design section of the current National Curriculum (DfEE, 1999) and 'Understanding the Arts' section of the curriculum (delete proposed) in Rose's Independent Review of the Curriculum (2009) and also the arts and creativity domain in the Cambridge Primary Review (Alexander, 2009). The emphasis in all three documents is on the exploration of colour, texture, shape, space and form in two and three dimensions and line and pattern, with ICT being of particular significance in the Independent

Review (Rose, 2009). The associated skills involve such things as drawing, painting, collage, sculpting and modelling, printing, using textiles, film and photography, and graphics.

Exploration

The word 'exploring' and its poll position in the title of this aspect of learning suggests it is key to understanding what the statement is about. It is a word packed full of educational connotations alluding to theories about play, active learning, constructivism, scientific enquiry and creativity, so in order to fully understand its intent, some knowledge and understanding about such theories would be undoubtedly helpful. Essentially, the aforesaid theories tend to inter-mingle in practice, along with others, so it is my intent to examine practice in order to show how these theories work in practice. Nevertheless, some funda-mental questions which the practitioner might ask when introducing oppor-tunities to explore are worth examining at this point; so to begin to examine what is meant by 'exploration', I am basing some of my ideas on Moyles' teach-ing strategies for active learning (1989: 20). There are other researchers in the field that provide similar models, for example, Harlen and Qualter (2004) 'process skills', Belle Wallace (2002) TASC model 'Thinking Actively in a Social Context'. Such models draw upon the ideas of Vygotsky and Bruner and are characterized by the central role of child–teacher, child–child interaction (see Mercer, 1995: 90).

The significance of choice

Moyles' model emphasizes the connections between play and learning theo-ries where play provides children with the active learning mode in which to explore, use and develop their skills, solve problems, practice skills and rehearse (1989). The first thing to consider is the context or *starting point* and how it is relevant to the child. Will the context interest the child? Will it stir within the child a sense of intrigue or stir the child's emotions such that the child will want to choose to enter the exploration? Choice matters and it starts early; one only has to think of the way in which very young babies discriminate between one weaning food and another to know this. Rich, Drummond and Myer (2008) consider choice highly significant and also refer to the early age when babies start exercising choice. One of the points they make that is particularly pertinent to this chapter is 'children exercising their power of choice whenever they act as designers, artists, builders, dancers, musicians, writers, actors, engineers, scientists, inventors and philosophers' (2008: 18). They make a case for the difference between *trivial choices* and *important choices* , the latter requiring practitioners to provide and organize for choice that leads to the child exercising *significant acts of judgement and reflection* thereby helping the child make informed choices (2008: 18). For example, a starting point for exploring colour might be set in the context of the school garden where the child has the opportunity to choose, collect, sort and talk about natural objects in relation to colour. Having said that, the child may well choose to pursue other things at this point and it is important that the practitioner be open to other lines of enquiry the child may choose to take. The more interesting the exploration is for the child, then the more likely the child will want to extend their response (Cooper and Sixsmith, 2003).

Christian Schiller (1979) identified the importance of choice for a child when talking about creativity at the HMI Primary Conference in 1965. He said that to be creative one must exercise personal individual choice. He went on to say that what we look for in creative work is not merely choice but feeling in the choice and he concludes his significant address by saying that when we sense and appreciate the feeling that went into the child's choice in effect we acknowledge and indeed should celebrate their creativity (1979/76). There are other implications for the practitioner, concerning starting points for learning. A most important aspect involves issues concerning inclusion, culture and diversity especially in relation to how these aspects affect the child's sense of choice. Furthermore, in the area of art and design what attracts one child may not attract another, in other words the subject matter can be very subjective and all the more reason for listening to the children, ensuring for inclusivity that also includes a child's culture.

Practical tasks

Look at your provision for exploration of media and materials. Observe children working in this area. How do you provide choice? Consider this in relation to choice of resources and choice of context. What sort of starting points are used and are these chosen by you or the child? How do you ensure that the starting points are meaningful for the children?

Alongside the thinking that is required to establish the context or starting point will be what you intend the child to learn, the *learning intentions*. Often the exploration will feature skills, but the knowledge and understanding that might be gained and the attitudes that might be promoted should be considered. Helping the child to develop positive attitudes to new things, and things that are initially different to expectations is crucial for the child's development to be holistic (see Broadhead et al., 2010). Attitude is a particularly significant aspect of exploration and one that can be a major driving force in holding a child's curiosity or not. I suggest that the idea of promoting positive attitudes is partly held in the word 'widening' used to qualify the phrase 'media and materials' in the EYFS statement, because increasing the breadth increases the opportunities for the child to meet new ideas and new issues. In the latest OfSTED report 'Drawing together' (OfSTED, 2009) there are two key recommendations, one to establish more differentiated starting points designed to develop skills, deepen knowledge and capitalize on the child's creativity and another, to ensure provision is relevant and wide-ranging, both capture the essence of my discussion so far and hopefully the chapter will suggest how this can be achieved.

Artistic purpose and exploration

It is important to give due attention to the artistic intent of the exploration. In the Rose Independent Review this artistic intent is termed 'artistic purpose' (2009: 193; DCSF, 2009) and identifies clearly the sort of activities the child should be involved in, which include 'making images and artefacts using appropriate tools e.g. brushes, sponges, crayons, rollers etc., and using materials including paper, card, textiles, clay, wire etc., and using ICT as a medium in itself and to explore other forms. This includes 2D and 3D and technologies such as computer art and graphics, animations, electronic compositions, videos and so on'. For the very young child exploring, or in other words playing, with such tools, media and materials is necessary and may or may not be for an outcome other than play. Through playing, the child develops mastery of the tools but initially the learning intention is for the child to play and to explore. Often the child will invent the purpose, for example, as play with crayons progresses and the marks take shape on the paper the child might then suggest what the drawing is about or invent a story as a result of the drawing. Invented narratives are a significant aspect of children's drawing and paintings that start to emerge at about the age of three and become a main drive in children drawing from then on (Matthews in Rodger, 2003). Abbott (2001: 18), in her book about the Reggio Emilia schools in Northern Italy, talks about children's love of weaving stories and the way in which they 'project' themselves into imaginary worlds, which is what many children do as they seek out the purpose of their early explorations of mark making in art. A problem with the notion of 'learning intentions' is the implied discrete nature of such an intention which in all likelihood will pertain to whether or not a child can hold a crayon and or make a mark with a crayon, which detracts from the overarching purpose of developing the artist in the child. Hence, there is a need for the practitioner to see beyond the immediate and to look to the 'artistic purpose' of the exploration.

Next is the *exploration* itself where decisions need to be taken on what media and materials to include, how they might be arranged, will there be adult help and what role will the adult play. At this point issues such as match and challenge matter. The young child needs lots of opportunities to play in order to practice and gain the skills. The element of challenge has to be carefully timed for each child so that it can be managed by the child and not cause the child to be overly frustrated which may lead to the child abandoning the challenge. Observations by practitioners provide the necessary information on the child's developing skills so that decisions can be made on how to take the next steps which might include one child showing another child what to do, or an adult supporting a child learning something new. The involvement of the adult leads to the next point for consideration which is – how does the adult know *when* best to support the child, *how* best to support the child and does the child need support. These types of questions are all about ownership, and require the practitioner to make wise and timely judgements such that intervention leads to independence and resourcefulness rather than be seen as an interruption or interference. Moyles (1989: 20) refers to intervention as 'adult value strategies' and in the questions she raises identifies the complexity associated with intervention, not least of which concerns what to say to the child in relation to sustaining motivation and interest while extending learning and without imposing value judgements which may or may not be appropriate or even right. The idea of when and when not to intervene relates directly to what is meant by 'children's independent and guided exploration', where the word independent suggests the child has gained some control over the media and material, possibly, having mastered some of the skills and possibly following some guided exploration. In other words, what level of support is needed and what will it look like. Part of this chapter will try to unpack what 'independent' and 'guided exploration' actually look like in the early-years setting.

Exploration and reflection

Exploration does not end there, the practitioner through observation and talking with the child *evaluates and analyses* what the child is learning and how the child is learning. While this *reflection* is critical for the practitioner in order to both review the child's learning and his or her own practice it is as important to involve the child in *reflecting* upon their experience too because it is through such talk that the practitioner becomes 'co-constructor' of the child's knowledge and understanding (Tough, 1976: 9; Mercer, 1995: 6; Abbott, 2001: 128). Language here is not just about communicating, but about being used to construct knowledge (see Callander and Nahmad-Williams, 2010). It is the part it plays in the child's intellectual and cognitive development (Vygotsky, 1962). Language that guides exploration in its fullest sense and which includes reflecting upon the experience changes passive exploration into active learning and enables the child to learn independently. In other words, the child, through shared talk, learns the language to learn.

Moyles' final strategy for active learning involves asking the question what kind of outcomes might be expected; she calls it 'justification'. To answer this we must return to the statement and look at it in its context of Aspects of Creative Development (DCSF, 2008) which remind us that creative development is not confined to art or indeed the arts but rather an aspect that cuts through subject divides. Children being children will affect our preconceived outcomes. As Tough (1976: 11) said 'the child's thinking is not like the adults', and importantly points out that the kind of thinking a child may express will be restricted by his level of understanding. The child's experience of exploration while providing the inner frames of reference from which language can develop (Piaget et al., 1969) is stimulated by the part others play in *scaffolding* the learning experience through talk (Mercer, 1995: 90). As I said earlier, when we talk to children we bring our own set of values; so what *we show to be worthwhile is likely to become worthwhile to the child* (Tough, 1976: 11). One example is of a nursery child who initially was quite reticent about joining in an activity exploring clay but became interested when the water started to flow over the table. The teacher asked the child how he would stop the water flowing away which led to an involved discussion about how to solve the problem. It is an example of the type of talk to which Mercer (1995) refers as constructing knowledge together and to which Alexander (2004: 28) calls 'cumulative dialogue' where the teacher and child build on their own and each other's ideas to form a chain of enquiry. I think this really raises questions about *our* expectations, in that do we limit the child's intellectual functioning by setting narrow outcomes and is the child's intellectual functioning also limited by interventions that fail to extend the child's understanding. The teacher could have easily mopped up the spillage and it takes an enlightened mind not to.

To further explore the issues discussed so far, I refer to a real example that happened in my classroom.

Case study

Some years ago when I was an infant teacher in an urban school I realized the significance of art in developing the curriculum that led to children working beyond my expectations for them, and as a consequence changed my whole outlook on how children learn. I remember being challenged by my class of 4- and 5-year-olds who during our topic on mini-beasts and after collecting some to look at in magnification boxes, then sketching from observation, one of the youngest children, Jamie aged 4, asked *why* insects have six legs. He was well aware that insects were defined by six legs but wanted to know *why* six and not eight like spiders or four like horses. His question arose from close observation and the conversations that were taking place between the children about whether or not they had the right number of legs on their drawings. This led the class on a quest to find out why, first by sorting different mini-beasts into groups. Quite by accident I had moved with the children into a science investigation, which challenged me to go beyond the expectations of the reception/year 1 class I was teaching. I could not ignore their suggestions and the ideas they put forward, including the suggestion that the first front two legs should really be called arms because the insects used them like hands to wash their faces. Here the children were observing closely for function and employing much higher order skills in Science than expected for children of their age, such as reasoning and deduction (see Cooper et al., 2010).

Two other boys David and Daniel, wanted to draw the mini-beasts all the time and each time I could see refinement and development in their drawing skills but I was aware of the time this was taking away from other areas of the curriculum, and constantly felt under pressure to re-direct them to other subjects from the drawing which had become so compelling. However, their skills were so appreciated by the other children that the other children's skills in drawing improved. Art wasn't a priority subject where assessment was concerned, certainly not in the same way as the Core by which the school was measured, but the evidence was so great in showing the way all the children's skills in drawing had progressed that I made assessment in art a priority for this topic. Through this topic I learnt much about learning and teaching, about being able to follow through children's ideas and justify my decisions. At the time of the mini-beast project, I had no so-called expertise in art but I became passionate about it because the children's skills in art, particularly close observation, led to more and more discoveries about mini-beasts as well as refinement of art skills, particularly those connected to line, pattern and form, aspects of art I had not envisaged at the start of the topic and which I had to learn about in order to talk about art at a more sophisticated level that better matched their rapidly developing skills and that encouraged the children to feel like artists.

Reflection for the early career professional

- Do you need to be an expert in art to become skilled in teaching art? Is passion enough? Consider what subject knowledge you feel you would need to promote artistic development in young children.
- What areas of expertise do you need for cross-curricular challenges?

Reflection for the leader/manager

- How can you justify outcomes that are unexpected? How would you support your staff with this issue?
- How will the value of the outcomes be communicated to others?

The 'why' question Jamie asked stayed with me and is an invaluable question to ask as one approaches new things, 'why am I doing what I am doing?' It is a particularly useful question to ask in relation to many tasks in school which seem to be routine such that when organizing for exploration we might think *why* this medium and *why* that material. It is important to know how provision meets both the immediate and discrete intentions for a child to appreciate and explore colour, texture, shape, form etc., but it is also important to be focused on the longer term gains to the child in terms of their development as artists. However, choosing what appear to be the appropriate materials for a particular activity may not always turn out as expected, on the contrary, it may well lead to unexpected outcomes that are the very essence of creativity. The remarks of one Miss Heale who was Inspector of the Board 1905, captures precisely such unexpected creativity when she reports that 'the best drawing I saw the Babies do was in sand – just a mouse, without any repetition' (HMSO, 1959: 215). And now, 104 years later OfSTED are saying the same thing when they report that 'The most effective primary art lessons were planned but did not prescribe the outcomes. The way that the teacher organised resources and used language invited choice, discovery and experimentation. Unexpected ideas from individual pupils were welcome and accidental effects celebrated' (OfSTED, 2009: 21).

Photograph 2.1 Art resources (© Emma Jordan)

Provision and progression

Have you ever been in a family situation where a young child has asked you to draw, and heard yourself responding with the words 'I'll have a go but I can't draw very well'? I am sure this request and response is familiar to many of us and when we do attempt to draw we feel a surge of inadequacy which does nothing to inspire a desire to learn to draw but rather make you wish you had learnt to draw at school. I do not think it unusual to find practitioners lacking confidence in art; indeed in the recent OfSTED report (2009: 20), a survey of primary school teachers showed that many of those surveyed said they lacked confidence in drawing. The report found that 'teachers, whose own artistic competence, whether acquired from their own education, through formal training or simply from an appreciation of art, was an important contributor to success' and that 'developing skills in the specific art form remains important'. So, we have practitioners recognizing their lack of confidence through a perceived lack of skill, together with OfSTED recognizing the importance of some baseline knowledge and skill in art as a prerequisite for success. It should be said that OfSTED raised concerns about limited professional development opportunities also, and recommended more opportunities for developing knowledge and skills in art through Continuing Professional Development provision. Certainly, if we value the role of shared talk in developing a child's knowledge and understanding, then the talk has to provide the artistic language upon which the child can build meaning. Therefore, the practitioner's knowledge about art has to be such that it can help scaffold the child's understanding.

Eglinton (2003) when addressing primary children's lack of confidence in art suggests that 'passive' approaches to art in the early years and the 'progressive' education movement which stressed the freedom to explore, has led to a non-interventionist approach or a 'passive approach' to art in the early years. Eglinton (2003: 11) argues the case for dialogic intervention so that children have the opportunity to talk about their experiences making art, as well as their appreciation of art at an early age. Her argument is that the central purpose for children exploring media and materials should be to develop their artistic skills in terms of helping them understand the materials and what they can do. It may be that both the practitioners' lack of confidence in drawing, and notions of non-interventionist approaches in early-years teaching are contributing factors to some primary children's lack of confidence. However, artistic competence or talent does not in itself guarantee effective art-teaching. Examples were seen where teachers did too much for their pupils, 'driven by their own vision of an end result' (OfSTED, 2009: 20).

Overall, the latest findings by OfSTED (2009: 4) are encouraging and would suggest that Eglinton's earlier claims have been somewhat addressed when they report on children's creative development as good in one half of Foundation Stage settings. However, they do report how easy it is to underestimate children's abilities to record observations and express imagination through mark making (2009: 8), which echoes a little of what Holt (1997) was saying in that there comes a point where exploration has to become something more. I believe practitioners know the value of talk in early learning but their negative perceptions about not being able to draw, suggest that shared talk might lack the language about art skills that enable children to make meaning of their explorations.

Starting points

I believe that greater understanding about provision and how this can impact on progression can go some way to alleviating practitioners' fears of not being able to draw, and knowing little about art. Provision is about the media and materials but is also about the firsthand experiences or starting points and contexts that we provide. Starting points, whether this be a walk around the school, visit to a local shop, a famous painting or a collection of objects etc., provide the stimulus from which the exploration can begin. Provision is also about the shared talk that accompanies the exploration and the more knowledge and understanding the practitioner gains about the starting points and their relationship to media and materials, the more expert the practitioner is likely to become in learning and teaching about art and the learning that occurs through art. One outstanding school I know, and have worked with over many years, has achieved its outstanding status because of a strong philosophy that provides a climate where learning can flourish, that is, in part, achieved by the significance given to the relationship between provision and progression. The Head Teacher states the importance of giving very young children time to practice and to come to terms with the DISCIPLINE of the materials BEFORE they become more controlled and this is an extremely important piece of learning for children in the early years. Each child is a record of their development, and spontaneous drawing of a very young child is a record of their contact with the world, just as surely as is the most technical diagrammatic drawing, which is very exact in scale and relationships done by an older child.

He achieves progression by ensuring first, that the children's starting points for learning are broad, exciting and inspirational. Secondly, the aim to provide children with experiences that can be deepened and extended determines the choice of materials in that the materials themselves are capable of being developed. The idea behind the school's policy for art is well founded in research addressing creativity, Sternberg (1999), Smith (1992) and of course, the Reggio Emillia preschools where, in the central 'atelier', artistic materials are set out uniformly so that the child can build knowledge of the materials and their potential. Throughout the school, from reception to year 6, the classes are resourced the same for painting, drawing including fabric, clay and printing and it is to this arrangement that I now turn my attention.

Painting

Painting lends itself to an exploration in colour for the child but the child first needs to explore the colours that they see around them. A teacher who helps the child see the vast range of hues and tones in the environment, and for example, the subtlety in differences between one fallen leaf and another, fosters within the child the curiosity to explore, discover and find for him/herself. Appreciating colour is the first step towards creating colour with paint. It is also the underlying reason why many practitioners advocate the use of powder paint so that children make their own colours thereby maximizing the potential for exploration. However, each type of paint medium whether powder paint, ready-mix paint, paint washes, water colours etc., have particular qualities and it is the practitioner who must decide which is best suited for the art activity. Ready-mix paints are the most difficult for the child to control because of their runniness, and also to mix, because of the rapidity of the mixing process which does not allow for subtle colour change. Moyles (1989: 77) refers to one such scenario where children were using ready-mix paints to paint chicks that had been brought into the classroom for the children to see. From the observations of the children she noted how difficult it was for them to re-create the colours. White had not been provided and so they could not capture the variety of tones of yellow. One child on going over to look once more at the chicks to check the colours in the eye could not create the variety of colours and, as all the brushes were large and already standing in the pots of colour, the child was drawn away from her creation and diverted to another. Moyles raises a number of questions but one in particular stands out in relation to points I made earlier about artistic intent. She asks how the teacher approaches the whole question of creativity in terms of artistic impression, which resonates with my point concerning the need to keep in mind the underlying reason for the explorations as well as the discrete learning that takes place.

Photograph 2.2a Picture of a child's painting (Edenthorpe Hall Primary School, Doncaster)

Case study

The following scenario is a recent one that occurred when I was working with a class teacher to support a group of four student teachers on a 2-week placement in their first year of training. The children in the reception class had been on a nature walk around the school to look how Autumn was affecting the colour of the leaves and to collect some colourful leaves. The ratio of adult to child was good so lots of shared talk took place with the adults supporting children and offering new words to describe the colours such as golden, amber, cherry, crimson. When the children returned to the classroom and following a lively class discussion about the colours of the leaves the children were directed to the activities, which included special painting activities to capture the colours they had seen, supervised by the students. Each painting table was set out for four children where each child had a piece of sugar paper, a tray with four pots of powder paint, white, yellow, blue and red, a water pot, a paint brush and a sponge for dabbing off excess water. The children were in their first term but had been introduced to powder paint and how to mix it, having

⇨

already explored how to make green from blue and yellow, orange from red and yellow and purple from red and blue. Each student worked with a group of four children.

What ensued was fascinating in that most children just wanted to mix paint where the dilemma for the students was how to encourage the children to make marks with the colours being made. However, mark making was low in order of priority for a goodly number of the children who were delighting in mixing and making new colours. The students encouraged the children to mix the paint to an appropriately thick consistency, to prevent the paint running on the paper, and to give texture to the brush strokes. During playtime, the class teacher and I and the students discussed what was happening, and in particular, the frustration the students felt because the children were not using the colours they had made to make marks, or capture the colours on paper. We talked about the value of the exploratory practice of mixing paint and making colours advising the students to make use of their notebooks to write down comments from the children that might reveal some of the learning that was occurring. The class teacher organized to take photographs of the children so that the exploration of mixing paints was recorded. The students asked me what they should say to the children as their conversations so far had been aimed at persuading the children to use the paint. I suggested they ask the children to think what was happening when they mixed two colours together. Also, to ask the children if they had seen the colour they had made before, and where and when. To encourage the children to talk about what their new colour reminded them of, and for the student to offer an analogy of their own (here I referred to the way in which lipsticks are named and suggested how useful such references to the familiar could be in order to encourage and extend conversation/dialogue). What followed was extraordinary mainly because it revealed to the students the worthiness of exploration of media and materials and that the end product was the child's learning. The following are a few of the comments arising from the shared talk that occurred. The students used the comments to accompany photographs of the children mixing paints for a learning wall display.

One little boy said when looking at his palette of primary colours:

> I can make all the colours in the world.

A little girl said:

> I made Auntie Mable's cardigan green.

A conversation between two children occurred:

> Child 1: If you keep mixing I wonder what will happen?
> Child 2: You shouldn't use a lot of water.

Case study—Cont'd

Child 1: Why?

Child 2: Because you'll lose the colours.

It is these snippets, or what used to be termed in early-years practice, 'noteworthy comments' that reveal the real value of the activity and serve as genuine pointers to the learning that is taking place.

Reflection for the early career professional

- How might you ensure that you make note of the children's talk during painting activities as well as assessing the painting produced?
- When children are painting, how do you ensure that they are able to mix and create colours that they want to use?

Reflection for the leader/manager

- Audit your painting resources. How do you ensure that children can explore colours through painting?
- Discuss the different opportunities your setting provides for painting and if these could be improved to allow for more dialogue during painting. How could these experiences be used to demonstrate progression?

Photograph 2.2b Picture of a child's painting (Edenthorpe Hall Primary School, Doncaster)

Matthews (1994) in his examination of young children's drawings, in particular his own children's development, believe that the child's main aim may not be to represent something but may simply reflect the child's absorption in the effects of his or her own movement or the effect of mixing colours (Smidt, 2002). Gentle (1993) drew attention to the way in which adults look mostly for results and tend to undervalue, overlook and even dismiss such activities. In his discussion about such *disparity between what children experience and what adults assume is happening* (1993: 1) he directs those working with young children to find ways and means of sharing experience. But, what does it mean to share an experience. Looking back at the scenario I described, the ingredient that was missing was the doing of the activity together, 'sharing the experience' and in so doing, child and adult discovering together. One has to be sensitive as to when to enter the child's territory, but starting out together on a journey of discovery such as mixing paints is one way of sharing experience such that the experience is of consequence to both the child and the adult.

Moyles (1989: 76) captures well the sometimes participatory role the practitioner has to play when she writes 'the role of the teacher must be in observing, initiating, participating, encouraging, maintaining and extending children's art experiences'. In the same chapter in her groundbreaking book on play she discusses the significance of providing children with 'the appropriate techniques and materials' (1989: 78) that enable the child to fully explore the 'potential' of the experience. For example, in the previous scenario the resources encouraged the mixing of paint, but think how having a choice of paper might have shifted the emphasis onto using the paint, similarly a collection of brushes. Selection and choice by their very nature suggest possibilities to the child, so in the same way that the child might have been thinking what will happen if I mix this colour with that colour, so the child might think I wonder what marks I can make with a thin brush, what will happen if I use a thick brush and so on. In other words, provision matters, because through tools, media and materials limits are set or possibilities created.

Drawing

This is probably the area where the practitioner feels least confident, but think of drawing as another opportunity for a shared experience with the child, drawing together. In my early years as a teacher I learnt to draw with the children, we learnt to look closely where the eye stayed with the object rather than the pencil, we learnt to draw from a point within the object rather than try to draw the outline and we learnt to improve through practice. Drawing with the children provides the practitioner with the opportunity to develop art skills of their own.

Once again provision matters and it is important that children are given resources that enable them to become good at drawing, so for example, a range of pencils with softer leads such as those in the range from 2B to 9B are much better for drawing and especially so for young children who need to be able to see they can achieve and are not put off by any frustration caused by inappropriate tools. Suitable pencils enable the child to experiment with shading, tone and texture. It is important that the child explores what drawing pencils can do and there is every reason for the practitioner to share the experience in the same way mixing paints can be a shared experience. I make no apologies providing high quality materials for young children, and also suggest that for best results, along with pencils, best quality cartridge paper should be used too, which when cut to appropriate sizes works out to be as economical as cheaper papers. Playing with pencils, making marks, creating lines and shapes should become part of a familiar repertoire for the young child rather than one off opportunities that cannot be developed.

In my reception classes I would collect each child's explorations with pencil, (and other mark makers including paint), to keep in a book of their drawings that was theirs for them to look at, and so we could talk about it together. It served as a portfolio of their developing skills but it was not primarily for assessment and stored away, but rather, used. Young children should not be underestimated when it comes to reviewing and reflecting upon their work, in this case their pictures. They learnt to appreciate their 'getting better' at drawing and were able to start to appreciate the efforts of their friends in relation to the pictures they created. Their book of pictures was used in the same way as little books I would construct for them containing their anecdotal stories that we could share together with other children in the class. Often the children were able to tell you where they created the picture, who was there with them, that their friend drew a picture too and so on. A significant aspect was the way their drawing developed into pretend writing and/or picture stories where the children were able to tell a story through their drawings, something I had experienced during my training when I was fortunate enough to work in schools in Rotherham and Doncaster with a strong tradition in child-centred learning and learning through the arts. OfSTED (2009: 9, para 21) continue to cite such pedagogy as best practice 'Drawing, in a variety of media, is associated with play and playfulness in early-years teaching. Children often tell stories through their drawings, talking about what is happening as they draw'. In my reception classes children would frequently use their pictures from which they could verbalize their narratives. The following two examples typify the type of narratives that occurred.

Case study

David, aged 4 drew a picture of himself in bed with a thermometer in his mouth, and a bedside table upon which was a glass with a straw. Only later in his retellings did I notice the capital letters that made up a vertical sign along one side of the picture that spelled MRSFOSTER (at first I thought the letters were a pattern) who was the school's classroom assistant and who looked after children when they felt poorly. The detail in David's picture helped David retell his personal story of being ill in school and the addition to the story of Mrs Foster's sign that had fallen down, hence its vertical position in the picture. David was able to embellish his story each time he told it, including one tale where the sign hit Mrs Foster on the head to which her response to David was 'I don't think so David, I'm still here!'

Joanne, another 4 year old in the same class, who was just starting to create recognizable images, painted a picture of a tree with a ring in its branches. From this she invented a story of a pony who could fly called Mary Dianne, who dropped the ring in the tree as she was flying to give it as a present to a fairy. Several stories emerged over a number of days about how the ring was recovered. She drew upon her knowledge of story often drawing on the nativity story and the nature of giving gifts. There was an even stronger analogy to the idea of quest and the trials and tribulations that occurred as Mary Dianne tried to retrieve the ring. Her one painting led to a myriad of invented stories.

Reflection for the early career professional

- What opportunities do you provide to encourage children to develop narratives from their drawings?
- What do you think are the advantages of enabling children to develop stories from their drawings?

> ## Case study—Cont'd
>
> ## Reflection for the leader/manager
>
> - Discuss with your staff how they respond to children's drawings? What sorts of opportunities are provided to enable children to use their drawings as a stimulus for developing stories?

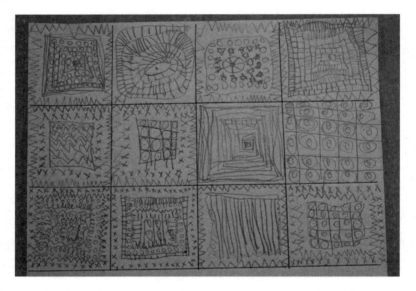

Photograph 2.3 Picture of a child's drawing (Edenthorpe Hall Primary School, Doncaster)

In the case study above, children were making meaning of their pictures by 'storying' (see Callander and Nahmad-Williams, 2010). Wells (1987) in his seminal work on children learning language and using language to learn says children construct stories in the mind as one of the most fundamental means of making meaning and, as such, it is an activity that pervades all aspects of learning (1987). It is important that children have opportunity to play at drawing rather than be limited to drawing by observation because through the playful experience of drawing young children have the means to express their imagination before being able to write or even tell stories. However, I want to expand a little by what I mean by observation at this point by returning to Schiller's address at the 1965 HMI Conference (Schiller, 1979), because he pointed out that there is more than one way of observing. Prior to him saying that he had likened the eye to a camera but observation, he went on, is more than that. To show this he drew on the way a child's attention which initially focused on, for example, a flower, shifts to focus more on the feelings aroused by observing the flower. So what begins as a drawing or a painting of a flower recorded by the 'camera eye' becomes part of the child as the drawing takes shape. This is what Schiller refers to as the 'you' quality which we call creative. He warns against too much objective observation but rather advocates the child's 'need to be able to observe along the whole gamut from creative observation at one end to objective observation at the other' (1979: 78).

Another reason for the children's inventiveness was the child's knowledge that their drawings and paintings were of value and had a permanence in the school community. Their artwork wasn't something that was 'done', it was seen as integral to learning and therefore something to be returned to. Drawings and pictures made up class storybooks which were told and retold and later words added to create books to read. Nearly 20 years later their picture books still exist having been used extensively in the teacher training programmes in which I am involved. Making marks is all about the child wanting to make some permanent mark on the world, rather like our ancestral cave painters who in their pictures told their stories of their awe, wonder and fear of the animal kingdom and their power over it (Breuil, *Cave Drawings*, 1954).

Drawing is not all about pencil; other mark making materials should be part of the provision that encourages children to make marks, such as already mentioned and others such as chalk, felt tip pens, wax crayons and pencil crayons. A child's weak pencil hold can partly be addressed by the addition of rubber pencil grips but much remains with the practitioner who helps position the fingers, provides the encouragement and provides vital activities alternative to drawing that strengthen grip and develop fine motor control. The practitioner's care cannot be overestimated and is central to developing skills in all children. It is a caring practitioner who knows how to 'guide exploration' without taking over.

Clay

Children from an early age enjoy exploring the properties and qualities of materials they can mould and make into different shapes such as playdough and plasticine, but clay has particular tactile qualities that make it an ideal medium for self-expression. Initially the child needs to explore clay and for this reason it should be as readily available in an early-years setting as paints and pencils. Playing with clay enables the child to handle shape and form which initially might be through rolling it, squeezing it, pinching it, poking it, to make different shapes. Through this type of play, the child can be guided towards making shapes and objects such as balls, bowls, fruit shapes etc. The value of making a clay model at this stage is not necessarily the end product but rather the process of finding out about the various aspects of the object. For example, from handling an orange, seeing it move, feeling the pattern on the skin etc., a child can then play with clay to create a model of the orange, using the hands and fingers to create its shape and tools to cut or pinch a pattern to look like the orange skin. All sorts of textures can be produced by pressing all kinds of objects into clay such as shells, stones, seed pods etc., and either using them to make a textured effect or leaving them in the clay. Making patterns in clay either with their fingers or with tools provides additional challenge that requires the child to be creative with the tools.

Exploring clay in the early years lays down the skills for modelling with clay, that pave the way for more sophisticated techniques in modelling such as coiling, slabbing and slip work later on. Trying out such sophisticated techniques too early can lead to frustration; so it is important to ensure that children's confidence with clay is secured. A colleague and sculptor, who I was fortunate enough to work with, felt that in many schools there is unbalanced provision of opportunities for children to engage in tactile activities. In the latest OfSTED report (2009) while the imbalance is not as evident as in previous OfSTED reports on art and design, emphasis is given to the success of boys as well as girls when tactile experiences are plentiful. Connolly suggests that the imbalance in broad terms favours verbal and written communication, in narrower terms it favours 2D activities which are a visually biased means of communication. Also, contemporary technologies of photography, film, TV, video, distance the child from the tactile and physical engagement with experience of the world. He argues that the communication of tactile experience is uniquely served by a medium such as clay where images and effects can be achieved without using visual judgements and makes the case that the blind and visually impaired are immediately empowered as communicators through the medium of clay (Connolly, 2001 unpublished). Whist the 3D tactile element is present in such activities as animation, which has become very popular in schools including infant schools, it is not the same as what Connolly is talking about where the sculpture itself is the means of communication.

In his attempt to demystify the medium he recommends, there should be at least one opportunity in every child's education to dig clay, prepare it, shape it and have this product fired, which he says is fairly easily done. I would not dispute this as from my experience of developing ponds in school grounds I have on a number of occasions involved the children in 'puddling clay' to secure a watertight base for the pond. Certainly, it is often possible to dig below the soil to reveal the clay substratum but this will depend on the geology of the area. Once you have the clay, continue to share with the children the process of making clay for using in the classroom. First, allow the clay to dry, then break off small pieces and place in a bucket or bowl to which water is added until the material thickens the water to a creamy consistency. Then pour the mixture through a sieve onto a porous surface such as a plaster mould or block and usually within half an hour there will be a layer of useable clay (Connolly, 2001).

Some teachers feel clay can be too messy but this is not what I have found. One of the most useful resources I made for children to work with clay was hessian-covered boards about the size of large breadboards. The beauty of the boards was the ease with which children could pop them onto a table and the hessian, which enabled the children to use the clay without it sticking to the surface. Also, once the boards had dried, excess clay could be brushed off making it ready for reuse. Involving children in the upkeep of the materials and tools used in the classroom is all part of the way in which children can be encouraged to take care of them. When considering the organization of resources, materials and media, it is useful if it is the same throughout so that children learn routines in preparation and tidying away in the early years that remain constant throughout the school. When organization varies from class to class the child has to spend time relearning dull routines, whereby his/her sense of autonomy is broken. For the child to feel totally autonomous within the school environment uniformity in the organization of resources is paramount.

Practical tasks

What different sorts of moulding material do you provide for the children in your setting? If you do not already use clay, consider trying out some of the ideas above. What skills are the children developing? What did you need to do to ensure the experience was successful?

Reflection for the early career professional

- What has the task highlighted in terms of organization?
- How do you ensure the resources allow for choice and autonomy?

Reflection for the leader/manager

- How do you ensure there is uniformity in the organization of resources in your setting?
- Discuss the differences between play dough and clay with your staff and identify the skills each one develops. When and why would you choose to give children clay to work with? When and why would you choose to give children play dough to work with? Are the reasons related to children's learning or adult needs?

Before leaving the topic of clay, and if my argument for its inclusion as a permanent feature of early-years settings and primary classrooms isn't enough, I return to the significance of its unique tactile qualities. It is through the tactile nature of clay that concepts about space, solidity and texture can be affirmed unlike 2D media. 3D work in clay accommodates such concepts more immediately and convincingly. The qualities of clay can satisfy the most urgent and expressive needs as well as more deliberate and subtle concepts. It allows modelling, construction and carving techniques to be developed as its plasticity changes in response to the stages of drying out.

Printing

Printing is the most forgiving of all the media I have discussed so far in that the printing process can make even the most elementary marks look superb.

It is a most wonderful means for exploring pattern, colour and shape. The child is particularly drawn to patterns, such as pattern in rhyme and dance, finger games, laying the table, lining up lego bricks and so on. Pattern is all around them, from bricks in a wall, rows of flowers in a garden, the layout of goods in the supermarket, upholstery, wall coverings and curtains. There are numerous patterns that repeat for the child to explore and with guidance, the child's sense of design can be developed. Robin Tanner (1904–1988) the artist and engraver in his book *Children's Work in Block Printing* (1970) is still by far one of the most useful books on printing because it not only addresses how to print with children but also why. He said, 'the whole business of pattern-printing is an intensely interesting game of arrangement, full of surprises, and producing shapes that have never been made before and that could not be made by any other means. Nor is there any end to the game, and its variations are countless' (p. 11). As with painting, drawing and clay, printing is a skill that can be progressed. Children's early explorations of printing soon lead to purposeful activities such as making greeting cards, place mats, curtains and table cloths for the role play area, book covers etc. Initially, very young children can use their fingers, the hand, toes and feet, to stamp out repeating patterns and begin to discover how to make colourful patterns on paper or cloth. Patterns with fingers can easily be created by dipping one finger in blue paint and another in red and stamping using alternate fingers. Altering the position of the finger, which is actually acting like a block, and stamping it onto the material is all the action needed for creating the print. There is so much scope for developing the artist and the craftsperson in the child through the processes of print that one has to question activities where the printing leads to a preconceived outcome on the part of the practitioner such as hand prints to make leaves for a class picture of a tree. Such activities limit learning, especially in this domain where the potential to develop artistic skill is so open. Using objects such as corks, twigs, stones, pebbles, shells etc., for printing offer more opportunities for exploration as not only has the child to consider colour for pattern but also shape for pattern. Successful printmaking is dependent upon good organization.

Like clay, all children should be able to experience the sense of success when exploring printing because the process is experimental whereby the whole idea is to try out possibilities and create alternatives. One of my student teachers when exploring printing in a college session wrote in her learning journal the following:

> I took a tube of paint and squeezed a generous amount into my palette. I then began to brush paint onto my leaf. Having done this I then firmly pressed it on a piece of paper and peeled it back slowly to reveal an interesting effect . . . Then I thought about how the shape of the leaf . . . my first thought was to rotate my template instead of placing it in the same position each time . . . then I began cutting up my template into sections to create depth as I lay down various coloured sections . . . I used my roller to mix up the colours . . . I discovered printing was not limiting as I first thought and that stunning effects can be achieved.

I wonder what we might think of a child who cuts up a template. In this student's case she could articulate the process of her exploration, something a child cannot do. I use her explanation as guidance for practitioners who may out of good intentions provide too much guidance and inadvertently interfere with the creative process rather than promote it.

Exploring printing techniques provides the child with opportunities to see things differently and from different perspectives. Only simple methods of printing in the early years should be tried, leaving more sophisticated forms until later. Potato printing is ideal for young children to try because very simple cutting and trimming can give an interesting shape, for example, a half moon shape by cutting the potato in half lengthways. Grooves can be easily cut into the potato to provide some complexity to the pattern, bold simple designs work best. This easy type of block potato printing allows the child to explore all manner of effects through, for example, rotating the block. Polystyrene tiles are ideal for press printing where an image or shape can be drawn onto the tile with something like a soft felt tip pen and then scored using a biro; when the design is finished paint can be rolled onto the surface ready for printing by pressing onto the paper, a clean roller rolled over the tile ensures that the print distributes colour equally over the paper. Mono printing is another technique where paint is rolled onto a sheet of Perspex upon which a piece of paper is placed and the image drawn with a pencil or biro. On this type of printing, include as much mark making as the child wants as this will produce an elaborate print. Place the print onto the paper and use a roller to press the print onto the paper.

Why painting, drawing, clay and printing?

Painting, drawing, clay and printing are the elements of art I have identified because each can be developed in its own right and it is important that the child build skills which can be used, transferred and applied. It is by no means an exhaustive list for instance textiles and a child's ability to use needle and thread is important, so too is the ability to create and compose on screen but I feel the skills associated with these chosen elements of art and design are somewhat universal. Neither should these elements exclude others for instance collage where the tearing and cutting experiences are so vital for fine motor skills and the sticking and placing so important for learning about composition. However, I have chosen them in part to show how skills can be built upon and how having skills widens the child's capacity to explore not just skills but ideas and issues because they have the means to represent these. The child, through explorations in paint, drawing, clay and printing, has the means by which to build skills and knowledge in art and design about colour, line, rhythm, shape, form, pattern, colour, tone, texture and composition, which in themselves are transferable.

While end product is not a focus for exploration, for children to make the artistic connections between why they are doing what they are doing then they need to see the products of the artists and to work with artists to see where it all leads. I have referred to the significance of the environment, how children need to explore the world around them in relation to art and design and starting points for art and design. Their environment should also embody the art and design work to which they might aspire and gain inspiration and include their own work which serves them in the same way. Children's explorations of media and materials should be celebrated and if appropriate displayed and used. Think about how artists' work is displayed and that should inform us of how to display children's work. If we are about awakening the artist in the child then we should let the child know they are artists and the way in which we display their art is a major signal to them in terms of how their art is valued. It is worth thinking about the means by which children can see the work of artists and designers and work with them, especially if we are to take up the recommondations of OfSTED and that is for 'every child to have the opportunity to work in an art gallery, or with an artist, craft worker and designer' (OfSTED, 2009: 6).

Developing an appreciation of art and design is equally important as learning art skills. It is through the appreciation of art and design that children see how skills are being used and applied. It is also worth thinking about what collections of artwork we might want for the preschool and school. Some can be remarkably easy to put together, for example, Tanner suggested a collection of William Morris simpler printed cottons such as 'Powdered Flowers', 'Strawberry Thief', 'Willow Bough' and 'Brother Rabbit' or some Morris wallpaper samples (1970). I have collected printed fabrics from around the world for my classrooms to show children printing's universality across cultures and the myriad of designs that can arise from such simple beginnings on a block. Children need to see the real thing rather than secondary sources. Photographs of painting cannot capture the texture or indeed the smell, and it is all these aspects the child needs to experience. Experience of the real thing is one of the reasons OfSTED advocate children working with artists and why Reggio Emilia schools have a resident artist or craftsperson as part of the atelier. Many local communities have artists and craftspeople who are more than willing to share their skills and work with children, some of whom might even be the parents of the children in your group. Indeed parents should not be overlooked, as often it is they who are the artists in the community but have never been asked, so it is just a matter of making contact. Secondary schools, colleges and universities, local arts groups, Local Authority collectives, are all avenues to try. It is a way too of embracing the cultures that make up a community and widening the child's experiences of culture and cultural art and design. Children need a wide range of art and design to explore from a range of cultures in order to appreciate other cultures and indeed cultures that make up their own community.

Guided exploration

I want to turn to the professionals' role. Media and materials are not enough on their own; children exploring is not a *passive* activity or solitary activity but one that should be shared. There will be times when children become so absorbed that they enter a world of their own which we have all seen happen and it is a time that should be respected, but on the whole children need lots of opportunities to co-construct knowledge and this requires the involvement of others (Mercer, 1995). Guided exploration is about sharing experiences where practitioner and child, in the same way as mother and child, partake jointly in exploration and experiencing new things together. Participation is about more than skills and knowledge about the exploration; it is about the affective domain because when sharing experiences such as being excited together, about discovering something new or trying out a new technique in printing etc., it is the emotions that are stimulated. Your participation, your reactions, your responses, your empathy, provide the means by which the child travels emotionally, it is in this, the affective domain, where attitudes begin to take shape and why your model is paramount.

As opportunity arises, teaching involves extending talk to co-construct knowledge (Mercer, 1995) which may involve just one child where the talk can lead into a line of enquiry for that child, but serves other children who are listening by demonstrating to them what extended talk or 'cumulative talk' looks like (Alexander, 2004: 28) . Guided exploration involves the practitioner in different aspects of teaching including participating, listening and responding to children, negotiating lines of enquiry. At appropriate times the practitioner will need to demonstrate new skills, but it is not just the technical skills the child needs, the affective domain is important and needs as much nurturing as the intellect. For example, in teaching about how to use brushes for painting, what different brushes can do, how artists used different brush strokes for different effects, it is important to consider how the brush is not just an instrument guided by the hand but an instrument guided by the 'heart', the 'imagination', the 'mind' . What might have guided Van Gogh to paint sunflowers or Moore to create the sculpture of the Fallen Warrior, is the aspect that is worthy of greater consideration, because like the child, something drew them, even compelled them, and what compels is very much concerned with the emotions.

Enriching experiences

Provision for painting, drawing, clay and printing is about learning to use tools, as we have seen the media itself plays an instrumental part in enriching the child's explorations. However, provision is also about providing children with enriching experiences because it is from an appreciation of what is experienced that the child will want to express those experiences. Drawing, painting and making with clay, printing, are the natural means by which to do this especially for a child who has yet to develop other means of expression such as talking and writing. The urge to represent, such as through drawing, develops out of experiences. It is the child's way of representing something that has happened and is real, or something that is imagined or felt. Ruskin said 'You can no more see twenty things worth seeing in an hour , than you can read twenty books worth reading in a day. Give little, but that little good and beautiful, and explain it thoroughly' (Barnes, 1985: 25) which embodies what is involved in providing enriching experiences and guiding exploration.

What is an enriching experience? Imagine being on holiday every day where you are seeing places for the first time, discovering new food, meeting new people, venturing off the beaten track and open to all the various serendipitous happenings that occur. It can be like this every day for the very young child because the child's disposition is poised for the exploration and discovery that every new day brings. In the hands of a loving practitioner, every day for the child should be as enriching as being on holiday. It takes a practitioner to be aware of the richness of the environment around the child and what is happening in the environment in order to show the child the detail that lies within it and the potential for further discovery and investigation. In this way the practitioner is helping the child to appreciate the beauty around him and the detail in the beauty. If the practitioner sees the flock of starlings, the robin on the bird table, the blackbird with a rowan berry in its mouth, the dog with one ear up and one ear down, the cat in the garden who sits in wait, the flowers that make up a rhododendron bloom and so on, then the child sees them and joins with the practitioner in his or her appreciation of them. By referring to the benefits the child can make to the environment he directs us to the issues that can arise and how the child's learning can be extended and how children can contribute to the environment. Of course, holidays and new things do not alone sustain us, indeed if the experience was so good then it is natural to want to return and dwell a bit longer. So it is for the child, the child needs the opportunities to return and return again whereby the relationship with the adult guides the child into a relationship with the environment and the initial experience is deepened.

Encouraging an appreciation of the environment is a first step to awakening the artist in the child which in the first place might be taken by the practitioner for the child but soon become steps taken together. It is the stage when the child is thinking: What can you show me? What can you do? Equally the practitioner is thinking: What can I show the child? What can I do for the child? By enabling the child to appreciate the environment and especially notice the detail in it, then the child is prepared to take more first steps by wanting to represent what is experienced.

Case study

I remember my own child after experiencing lots of balloons around him at his first birthday party, learning to say 'bloon' which he said on what seemed to be a minute by minute basis. Consequently, in his high chair eating porridge for breakfast he would say 'bloon' and I would draw a circle in his porridge and then he would try and eat the 'bloon'. This became a regular happening whenever we ate. Also his grandparents would spend time drawing different coloured balloons for him with coloured pencils, and all the time Robert would watch and say 'bloon gen' (balloon again). In effect, all of this activity was serving as the scaffolding for Robert to be able to draw the balloons himself. It was not long before he was taking over from his grandparents and drawing his own balloons; these were the first marks he made and one could tell they were circles.

Reflection for the early career professional

- Can you think of examples where children have had a new experience and this has been developed using a range of media and materials?
- How might you scaffold children's new experiences leading to artwork?

Reflection for the leader/manager

- How are children's diverse range of interests catered for in your setting in terms of artwork?
- What scaffolding activities have you observed your staff doing with children to support the use of media and materials?

While there are recognized stages in the development of young children's drawing one cannot ignore the significant influence a carer and a practitioner can have on that development. Vygotsky argued that all human beings, even the youngest infants, are social beings and children develop through interaction with others. His argument went further and suggested that development proceeds from the social to the individual (Flanagan, 2005: 3). His thinking set in motion the development of socio-cultural and socio-constructivist theories that have made a major impact on pedagogy where greater emphasis has been given to the role of the adult, child/child interaction and group talk in particular. However, the enriched experience lies in the relationships between child and practitioner or child and carer and it is this that is significant to learning and achievement. The inspirational organization of the Reggio Emilia preschools is designed for the child to be part of the whole community. Making the community special is the atelier, which is a special space, like an artist's studio, that forms the philosophical hub of the community. In the atelier children and teachers work together to construct visual languages through which ideas and meanings are communicated and guided by the atelierista, the artist, artisan, whose purpose is to guide and extend creativity in the community. I think the interesting aspect is the way in which Malaguzzi saw the significance of the child to the community, by recognizing children's contribution to shaping it. He says 'to learn and relearn together is our line of work' (Abbott, 2001: 76). His philosophy very much embraces the importance of relationships, of revisiting experiences together. The environment alone is not enough, it takes a guiding hand or indeed hands, to deepen and enrich the experience and most importantly the child's hands that bring new insights and creativity to the experience.

A close look at progression

For clarity, I refer to babyhood to mean the birth to 4 months even though the helpless state is longer and therefore when I use the term baby it refers to this period. At about 4 months I refer to the baby as child because it is around this time that the child exhibits greater interactivity with the wider environment due to the rapid development in motor skills such as grasping, moving objects from hand to hand, sitting up and rolling. I acknowledge too the six stages of child development as in the Child Development Overview in the Early Years Foundation Stage (DCSF, 2008).

We expect to do things for babies because they cannot do things for themselves and we intrinsically know that in our 'doing' for the baby, the baby will learn to do things itself. There is a complex path to tread and a fine balance to achieve for the caregiver who begins by doing everything, to gradually hand over. Mainly by intuition and instinct the caregiver makes safe the path for the baby to make its transition from babyhood to childhood, recognizing, right from the very early stages of babyhood, the baby's desire to learn. Even in the so-called helpless state, when the child cannot survive unaided, Donaldson argued 'that human babies show signs of a strong urge to master the environment' (1978: 110). A child learns from experiencing not only what the carer does but what the carer sees, hears, tastes and feels, their experiences are mutual and the child seeks to enjoy them over and over again as part of the desire to learn. For example, it is not uncommon to see a baby of 6 months offering their comforter to the carer for the comforter to be offered back by the carer, the baby having learnt to enjoy the reciprocity of this repeated action. Just as the carer can encourage the child to develop social skills, language and number through songs and rhymes, so it is that the caregiver can encourage the child to become 'art rich' and skilful in art. There are several aspects in encouraging babies and young children to become art rich and skilful. The baby in the first instance wants to see and know the person who is closest to it. If you watch a very young baby you will see it constantly raising its hand to the carer's face and just as often see the carer with the baby's hand in their mouth encouraging the baby in its exploration of the human face. Exchanges in various amounts of nuzzling might occur, and the baby will push their hand along the face, the nose and eyes as the carer encourages the baby with the loving responses and gestures. In the first 2 months the baby's sight is the weakest of its senses, so relies upon other senses, especially touch. In this way the baby gets to know the detail of the face and by the end of 2 months is exploring the faces of others close to it. Not surprisingly a baby chooses to look at a face over and above anything else or any other shape. By 6 months the child is drawn to the faces of other babies, and by 12 months the baby is able to understand expressions. It follows that one of the first things to emerge from a young child's scribbles is the shape of the human face.

The development of drawing is well documented in Kellogg (1969) and Matthews (1994). However, in my career in early-years education I have always been struck by the number of children who exceed the expectations in such models and equally the number who do not. I have found that much depends upon the opportunities the child is given and the support from the adult and also the home environment. Children who see adults drawing, painting, making models just as they see adults using computers will want to emulate what they see, indeed many young children come to school as experts in handling computers because computers in the home are more commonplace than other creative forms.

Recently, in a nursery foundation stage classroom, I worked alongside two girls aged 3 with the intent of observing the type of art activities they engaged in specifically looking for drawing skills. Matthews suggests in his model that between the ages of 3 and 4 children's symbolic representation is emerging and they experiment with a variety of marks using different materials and tools, draw circles plus lines to represent a person and start to produce visual narratives. The following is a description of what I observed.

Case study

The room was set out with a permanent site for exploring drawing media and materials. Additional to the drawing site were permanent sites for computer activities where the program was one for children to click on colours and shapes to make a picture, and a cutting and sticking site. Large boards were positioned inside and outside for the children to use felt tips and chalks. The morning session was organized such that children worked with their practitioners in small groups for number and communication activities, and practitioners supported the children in activities the children selected both indoors and outdoors. One of the girls, following her group activity, chose to draw whereupon I sat with her following approving smiles and the offer of coloured pencils which I felt confirmed her approval of my joining her. She began to draw a wonderful flattened circle which she drew from left to right adding two straight lines which confirmed it a person, it transpired it was her dad. Her additions to the drawing led the conversation which she often initiated but the quiet way in which she did this set the tone for the conversation which was conservative and subdued and I did not try to change this but rather was happy to be led by it. The detail she added was a thick stripe running down the side of the face, and a line of dots alongside the stripe, 'my dad's computer' she said. I was thinking they were trees and flowers so I was pleased that I did not intervene with my ideas at this point. Other detail followed including eyes and a huge smiling mouth. I noticed at the next activity time she chose to add more to her drawing and sought me out to join her. This session was very short before she was called away for outdoor activities. One has to ask what this says about the initial level of interest she exerted, the sustained interest she demonstrated by her returning to the activity and adding to the picture, and also seeking out my involvement.

The other girl I observed chose the computer where she was happy to discover for herself how to construct a picture. I noticed that the frantic clicking of the mouse offered success in that at some point a click was bound to cause something to happen such as to colour the background blue, but she was not aware of how to achieve a successful operation other than relying on chance. I felt I could support her by helping her to slow the process down so that she could see what effect a click of the mouse caused. However, it was very evident that she was not ready for that sort of intervention at this point because she was enjoying, what was to her, being in control over the computer. Was I right not to intervene at this moment in time? She was then drawn away from the computer for fruit time. When this was over she joined me at the drawing table to see what was happening, she said she could draw a cat and proceeded to select a blue pencil crayon to first draw three dots arranged like a triangle. She then drew a rectangular shape underneath the two dots that made the bottom of the triangle, adding two lines 'for legs' she said. When she said this I saw the cat which I couldn't make out before. She then said 'and there's its tail' while drawing a curved line away from the body of the cat. At this point I asked her if she had a cat to which she replied no and skipped off to do something else.

Reflection for the early career professional

- How might you have encouraged the child to initiate further drawing activities?
- Should you provide focus for the drawing activity and if so, how could this be achieved?
- What do you have to know about children's development in drawing in order to record progression?

Reflection for the leader/manager

- What experiences are you offering that involve the child in using all their senses?
- What other activities might impact on drawing skills and what other activities provide a means for the child to represent their experiences?
- Do your staff know enough about dialogue and the very young child such that intervention supports but does not overwhelm or take over?
- How well and how much are you and your staff using the wider environment, including the cultural environment, to foster an appreciation of the beauty and the detail that surrounds the child?

Conclusion

Each child's experiences of exploring materials and media in art and design will differ and for many their experiences before entering nursery or school will be limited. Similarly, their experiences of the natural environment and the local community, where so much stimuli for art and design lies, may also be limited and for them the process of enriching their lives by simply exploring new things is paramount. As a consequence of the child's prior experiences or lack of them, the timeliness of when to engage the child in talk relies heavily upon the expert judgement of the practitioner and his/her knowledge of the child. Most children require the time to exercise all their senses when exploring new things before talking about their experience, especially if they are aware of some inadequacy in themselves. I have found that even very young children intuitively pick up on the expectations of those around them, they see how other children react and how adults react to them, and quickly determine what reaction is approved of or not, and as a consequence the situation can either fuel their curiosity or turn it off. It is an empathetic and wise practitioner who knows when to and when not to interact and intervene. Also, one has to account for the child's need to be totally absorbed, engrossed in their own world where the capacity to dwell and linger is greater than the desire to interact. Being absorbed is that state of being where play is at its most powerful. Play is the child's world and for a long time the child needs to 'just play'.

Bibliography

Abbott, L. and Nutbrown, C. (2001) *Experiencing Reggio Emilia Implications for Pre-School Provision.* Buckingham: Open University Press

Alexander, R. (2004) *Towards Dialogic Teaching Rethinking Classroom Talk.* 3rd Edition. North Yorkshire: Dialogos

Alexander, R. (2009) *Cambridge Primary Review.* Cambridge: University of Cambridge and Esmee Fairbairn

Barnes, J. (1985) *Ruskin in Sheffield.* Sheffield: Sheffield Arts and Museums Department

Breuil Abbe (1954) *Cave Drawings.* The Arts Council. Brown Knight and Truscott Limited and The Westerham Press Limited

Broadhead, P., Johnston, J., Tobbell, C. and Woolley, R. (2010) *Personal, Social and Emotional Development.* London: Continuum

Bruce, T. (1987) *Early Childhood Education.* London: Hodder and Stoughton

Callander, N. and Nahmad-Williams, L. (2010) *Communication, Language and Literacy*. London: Continuum

Collins, J., Insley, K. and Soler, J. (2001) *Developing Pedagogy Researching Practice*. London: The Open University. Paul Chapman Publishing

Connolly, J. (2001) *A Day with Clay. A Handout for Students*. Lincoln: Bishop Grosseteste University College Lincoln

Cooper, H. and Sixmith, C. (2003) *Teaching Across the Early Years 3–7*. London: RoutledgeFarmer

Cooper, L., Johnston, J., Rotchell, E. and Woolley, R. (2010) *Knowledge and Understanding of the World*. London: Continuum

DCSF (2008) *Practice Guidance for the Early Years Foundation Stage*. Nottingham: Department for Education and Skills

DfEE/QCA (1999) *The National Curriculum for England*. London: DfEE/QCA

Donaldson, M. (1978) *Children's Minds*. London: Fontana

Eglinton, K. A. (2003) *Art in the Early Years*. New York: RoutledgeFalme

Flanagan, M. (2005) 'Sociocultural Processes of Learning in Art among Early Years Learners'. Paper Presented at the British Educational Research Association Conference, University of Glamorgan, 14–17 September 2005. www.leeds.ac.uk/educo/documents/143470.htm

Gentle, K. (1993) *Teaching Painting in the Primary School*. London: Cassell

Harlen, W. and Qualter, A. (2004) *The Teaching of Science in Primary Schools*. 4th Edition. London: David Fulton Publishers

Hart, S., Dixon, A., Drummond, M. J. and McIntyre, D. (2004) *Learning without Limits*. Maidenhead: Open University Press

HMSO (1959) *Primary Education*. London: HMSO

Holt, D. (1997) 'Problems in Primary Art: Some Reflections on the Need for a New Approach in the Early Years'. *International Journal of Early Years Education*. Vol. 5, No. 2: 93–100

Joicey, H. B. (1986) *An Eye On The Environment: an Art Education Project*. London: Bell and Hyman in association with the WWF

Kellogg, R. (1969) *Analysing Children's Art*. Palo Alto, CA: National Books

Matthews, J. (1994) *Helping Children to Draw and Paint in the Early Years*. London: Hodder and Stroughton

Mercer, N. (1995) *The Guided Construction of Knowledge. Talk amongst Teachers and Learners*. Clevedon: Multilingual Matters Ltd

Moyles, J. R. (1989) *Just Playing? The Role and Structures of Play in Early Childhood Education*. Milton Keynes: Open University Press

OfSTED (2009) *Drawing Together: Art, Craft and Design in Schools*. London: OfSTED

OfSTED (2003) *Expecting the Unexpected. Developing Creativity in Primary and Secondary Schools*. London: OfSTED

Piaget, J., Piaget, L. and Inhelder, B. (1969) *The Psychology of the Child*. |London: Routledge and Kegan Paul

Rich, R., Drummond, M. J. and Myer, C. (2008) *Learning: What Matters to Children*. Clopton, Suffolk: Rich Learning Opportunities

Rogder, R. (2003) *Planning an Appropriate Curriculum for the Under Fives.* 2nd Edition. London: David Fulton Publishers Ltd

Rose, J. (2009) *The Independent Review of the Primary Curriculum: Final Report.* Nottingham: DCSF

Schiller, C. (1979) *Christian Schiller in His Own Words.* London: A and C Black

Smidt, S. (2002) *A Guide to Early Years Practice.* 2nd Edition. London: RoutledgeFarmer

Smith, F. (1992) *To Think in Language, Learning and Education.* London: Routledge

Sternberg, R. J. (1999) *Handbook of Creativity.* Cambridge: Cambridge University Press

Tanner, R. (1970) *Children's Work in Block Printing.* 6th Edition. Leicester: Reeves Dryad Press

Tough, J. (1976) *Listening To Children Talking. A Guide to the Appraisal of Children's Use of Language.* Leicester: Ward Lock Educational

Vygotsky, L. S. (1962) *Thought and Language.* Cambridge, MA: MIT Press

Wallace, B. (2002) *Teaching Thinking Skills Across the Early Years. A Practical Approach for Children Aged 4–7.* London: David Fulton Publishers

Wells, G. (1987) *The Meaning Makers. Children Learning Language and Using Language to Learn.* London: Hodder and Stoughton

Creating Music and Dance 3

Introduction

What is music?

Music is a powerful, unique form of communication that can change the way pupils feel, think and act. It brings together intellect and feeling and enables personal expression, reflection and emotional development. As an integral part of culture, past and present, it helps pupils understand themselves and relate to others, forging important links between the home, school and the wider world.

(DfEE/QCA, 1999: 14)

This statement from the National Curriculum demonstrates what an important part music can play in the development of the whole child. Music is both about the sounds we hear and the sounds we make. The sounds we hear might be professionally produced music but it might also be everyday or natural sounds, such as the sound of a train passing or wind blowing through the trees. Whatever the source of the music, it consists of different elements:

- Pitch (how high or low the sound is; this produces the melody);
- Rhythm (the length of the notes and the patterns they make);
- Tempo (how fast or slow the music is; steady or changing);
- Timbre (the type or quality of the sound, for example, an oboe and a trumpet sound very different);
- Texture (the way the sounds are layered);
- Dynamics (how loud or quiet the sounds are, including silence).

In composed music, these elements are combined in structures. We can engage with music through listening, performing, composing and appraising (DfEE, 1999).

Music has been a part of cultures throughout the world and throughout history. The earliest music was probably vocal accompanied by body percussion, before moving on to simple percussion instruments. Archaeologists have found flutes made from hollowed out bird bones in the Neolithic period, while an even earlier find made from a hollowed out bear bone may have been a Neanderthal flute (Zhang et al., 1999). A region's music is still one of the defining aspects of its culture. We use music for special occasions – no birthday party is complete in this culture without 'Happy Birthday to You' – but we also use it on a daily basis, listening to music on the radio, singing lullabies to babies. There are many different styles of music and purposes for music. There is formal music, like symphonies in concert halls and informal music, like skipping chants on the playground. There is music for listening to, like jazz in a club, music for joining in, like Kareoke in a pub, and music just to be performed for yourself, like singing in the shower. Most religions have sacred music to help believers understand and celebrate the divine. Folk songs pass on the stories of the people. Lullabies help children go to sleep. National anthems stir feelings of pride when performed for the gold medalist at the Olympics. Both the EYFS (DCSF, 2008) and the National Curriculum

(DfEE, 1999) are designed to help introduce children to this breadth of musical experiences.

What is dance?

All dance is movement but not all movement is dance.

(Davies, 2003: 181)

What makes a particular movement or collection of movements into a dance? It is common for dance to be accompanied by music. The title 'creating music and dance' reinforces this association between dance and music. However, not all dance is accompanied by music. Many modern dances are performed in silence, with the sounds made by the dancers as the only accompaniment. Sometimes this fusion of the movement and sounds of the dancers is a vital part of the performance, such as in tap dancing, clogging, Japanese Taiko drumming or the popular dance troupe Stomp.

Dance may involve the sort of role-play and imagination shown through movement that will be discussed in the next chapter. Dance also involves the combination of decision making, physical skills and spatial awareness discussed in the 'Movement and Space' chapter of the *Physical Development* book in this series. This blurring between dance, role-play and other forms of physical education exists in society as well as in schools. Indian Classical dance and many ballets tell stories through movement and gesture, with the dancers in role. There is considerable overlap between dance and gymnastics in floor routines and rhythmic gymnastics; between dance and ice-skating in the long program and ice dances; between dance and swimming in synchronized swimming. Many dance forms, such as jive and break dancing are both athletic and gymnastic in nature.

Dance has many forms and purposes and is an important part of a region's culture. There are formal and informal dances. Dances may be simple, like Auld Lang Syne, or complex, like may pole dancing. Some are meant to be performed by professionals while watched by an audience, while others are for everyone to join in. They may represent 'high culture', such as ballet, or everyday culture, such as the Hokey Cokey performed at parties. They may be highly structured, like line dancing, or free form, like modern interpretive dance.

In the end, perhaps whether or not a particular movement qualifies as dance is down to the intention of the dancer.

Photograph 3.1 Dancing (© P. Hopkins)

The development of music and dance

Unique child

The development of both music and dance are dependent on the child's global development. Physical development has a major impact. The child needs to develop gross motor control of arms and legs to make initial dance movements. These movements become more precise and involve more body parts as the child develops. To play percussion the child needs control of arms, hands and fingers. To sing the child needs to develop control of vocal chords, lips, tongue and mouth. Language development also plays a part in singing as the child learns to form specific sounds. Social development is also important as the child moves from music and dance being purely individual experiences to performing as part of a group. The EYFS (2008) theme Unique Child emphasizes that each child's development will be different and may be uneven across the different aspects. This must be considered carefully when planning music and dance for your children.

Positive relationships

One of the reasons that some adults are uncomfortable teaching music and dance is that they feel self-conscious and exposed when performing. As part of the EYFS (2008). Positive Relationships theme it is important that you encourage the children to feel confident and secure when performing, by valuing their efforts, encouraging experimentation and demonstrating that they should respect each other. This emotional environment is an important factor in developing children's attitudes to music and dance, as well as their skills and knowledge. There are many implications for the physical environment as well, which will be discussed further later in the chapter.

Musical activities

Listening and appraising

As was stated above, music can be engaged with through listening, appraising, performing and composing. These areas are interlinked and all need to be developed. Listening is the most fundamental component in any musical activity and the one that adults do most often. Singing, playing, improvising and composing are dependent on the children's ability to engage in a listening experience that will help them to analyse, appreciate and understand what is going on in music. In order for this 'meaning-making' to take place, there needs to be opportunities for purposeful listening which leads to appraising, as opposed to just hearing music in the background. Listening to music in a focused way has wider educational benefits because it helps teach children how to listen and concentrate in other lessons (OfSTED, 2009: 12).

One way to appraise music is to talk with the children about what they hear. You should help them to make observations about other people's music, as well as making observations and decisions about their own music. However, children's ability to interpret music may well be in advance of their language development. As well as talking about music, children should be given opportunities to respond to music through movement, through choosing and creating visual images and by making their own music. Listening and appraising will inform their understanding, enabling them to refine, amend, adapt, reject, extend or transform ideas when composing.

When choosing music for the children to listen to, try to provide a broad musical diet. This can include music from other countries and other times but also a range of music from here and now: traditional children's songs, folk, jazz, blues, brass band, big band, pop, rock, classical, opera, musicals, country, bluegrass, rap etc. Before using any music listen carefully to the lyrics (if any) to make sure they are suitable for young ears. My research into children's listening preferences (Compton, 1999) showed that children in Reception and Key Stage 1 were open-minded listeners and were particularly receptive to a range of styles. If the children become acquainted with a large range of styles when they are young they tend to be more receptive to new music when they are older. I have noticed an increasing tendency for children's CDs to give a pop feel to traditional songs and nursery rhymes, presumably in belief that this will make them more appealing. While I did find that the majority of children enjoyed pop music, they liked other styles as well. I think that the production quality is a more important consideration. When you are playing music for the children to listen to, you need to keep the excerpts quite short, 1 to 2 minutes, unless the children will be actively responding to it through movement or creating art. I would recommend using music that you like since the children will usually pick up on your reactions.

Case study

2-year-old at home

We sometimes play music during dinner. One night we put on Louis Armstrong. Pippa, 28 months, said 'Oh thank you!' when the music started. She liked the bouncy New Orleans jazz numbers. However, when it got to St James Infirmary, a more bluesy number, she asked us to change it. When we asked her why, she explained that the music was too sad. After that we discussed the emotions for each song as it came up. She consistently asked to skip over the sad ones, but once dinner was finished she asked to hear the first song again so that she could dance to it.

Reception class

I made a collection of large pictures from old calendars and stuck them on a wall. The pictures included landscapes, animals, flowers, illustrations from children's books and pictures by famous artists such as Van Gogh, Kandinsky, Monet, Klimt and Picasso. The Reception children sat on the carpet where they could see the

⇨

pictures. I played them three short excerpts of music, about 1 minute each. Every time the children had to choose which picture they felt best represented the music and then explain why they had chosen that picture. I emphasized that it was okay for them to pick different pictures because it all depended on how they interpreted the music and the image. We also discussed the fact that some children had chosen the same picture but for different reasons because they were focusing on different elements of the music or different aspects of the image. After listening to the three pieces, the children worked in small groups to compose their own music based on one of the pictures. They performed them for each other. The listeners gave feedback to the musicians and said how they felt the music went with the picture. The composers then explained how they had used the picture to make the music.

Year 1 class

The Year 1 class were in the hall for a dance lesson. After a warm-up they focused on one body part at a time, moving that part of the body in different ways in response to the music. The music was a sampler CD that had short excerpts of music from around the world, different times and different styles. For each body part three children were chosen to watch the others and pick out movements that were particularly interesting, which the children were then asked to demonstrate to the rest of the group. The teacher commented on how certain changes in the music resulted in certain types of movement. The children were asked to describe what aspects influenced them and how that affected the quality of the movement (i.e. strong, light, explosive, smooth etc.). Over the next two lessons the children created their own contrasting dances in small groups in response to Soul Limbo (the BBC cricket music) and a steel pan version of Island in the Sun, focusing on how the differences in the two pieces influenced differences in movement.

Reflection for the early career professional

- When you use music, is it just in the background or are the children actively listening to it?
- When you listen to music, in what ways do you get children to respond to it?
- How do you choose what music you provide for the children to listen to?

Reflection for the leader/manager

- How do you ensure progression in music and dance activities?

> ## Case study—Cont'd
>
> - When children are responding to music how can you ensure they present their own opinion rather than copying what others do or say?
> - How do you support children who have difficulty focusing enough to listen?

Composing

Composing allows the child to demonstrate independence and decision making. Many adults are scared by the thought of composing with children, thinking that composition means symphonies by Beethoven. However, the composing process can be much simpler than this. It starts with improvising (experimenting with sounds) and leads to composing (making decisions about sounds). These decisions can be as simple as when to play and when not to play an instrument or what name to choose when playing a circle game. Through performing and improvising the children can build up a repertoire of sound and note patterns they can use for more deliberate compositions. Early work in this area may involve gaining confidence in imitating or echoing sounds and question and answer games in which the child is encouraged to make an individual response. Exploration of sounds, both vocal and instrumental, provides knowledge and understanding of their nature and how they can be used. The child's ability to control these sounds skilfully and sensitively, and to organize them within a musical structure, forms the basis of creative musical activity.

Performing

Performing includes singing and playing instruments. Singing is a fundamental musical activity. The composer Howard Goodall describes singing as '. . . one of the most culturally diverse and adaptable artistic activities' (Music Manifesto, 2006: 34). The voice is a versatile instrument that is free, always available and used by all cultures. In singing, the music is internalized because the person is making the sound directly rather than using an instrument to make a sound, so it is a whole body experience. Singing fosters aural skills and can be used as a foundation for instrumental work. Although singing can take place alone, it is often a communal activity, developing collaboration and a sense of team work. The Music Manifesto (2006) is championing group singing, recommending that children in the Early Years and Key Stage 1 take part regularly in whole class and whole school singing. Group singing has many benefits. In addition to the social benefits of being part of a group with a common aim, it has musical benefits. Large groups of children usually sing more tunefully than individuals or small groups. This is partly because the larger numbers make people feel more secure and confident and partly because they are listening to those around them and unconsciously trying to match the pitch. People who are confident often sing more in tune because they have better posture, open their mouths more and provide better breath support. The disadvantage of group singing is the reduction in creativity because the group is trying to conform and work as a cohesive whole. There may be overall creativity in the performance but this tends to be the creativity of the leader rather than of the individuals.

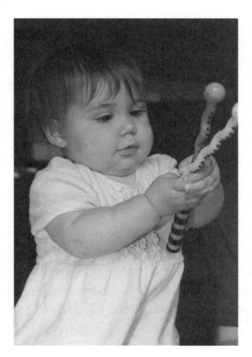

Photograph 3.2 Drumsticks (© P. Hopkins)

Performing can also take place on instruments, which most children enjoy. Performing on tuned and untuned percussion instruments contributes to children's understanding of rhythm, pitch, tempo, structure, style, dynamics, texture and timbre, as well as helping with the development of fine and gross motor skills. Performing with instruments requires many creative decisions from the children. They need to decide both when and how they are going to play, considering all the elements listed above. As they acquire greater competency on classroom percussion instruments, some children may be motivated to learn other tuned instruments, such as recorders, guitars and orchestral instruments.

The elements of dance

Just as music can be split into four activities, dance is often divided into four aspects. However, there is a lack of agreement about what these are.

Sexton (2004: 9, 10) refers to 4 components of dance:

1 Action – travelling, turning, gesture, stillness, elevation (e.g. jump), falling;
2 Space – level, direction, plane;
3 Time – speed and duration;
4 Dynamics – how these work together; the quality of the movement.

There is some overlap with Hall (2002: 6) who splits planning for dance into 4 stages:

1 The body – body parts, body shapes and the actions they make;
2 The space – direction, level and size of movement;
3 The quality – the weight or effort and the time or speed;
4 The relationships – alone, with a partner, in a group, the teacher.

He recommends focusing on one of these aspects at a time during the lesson, gradually putting them together. Lipscomb (2000) has a comparable set of four: body, space, weight and time; Davies (2003) uses some of the same words as Sexton and some the same as Hall: body, dynamics, space and relationships. Sabin (2002: 16) uses 4 questions instead, which could be answered by Hall's stages:

1 What is the body doing?
2 How is the body moving?

3 Where are the movements going to be performed?
4 With whom or what is the action performed?

The question approach is probably the easiest one for teachers to think about when planning, but it is important to remember the range of options that potentially answer each question. However, for the rest of this section I am going to use Hall's stages.

The body

Focusing on individual body parts helps young children to identify different parts of themselves, learn to name them, explore what they can do and develop control over them. This is particularly important in the early years but will continue to develop throughout primary school and beyond, especially as the body changes during puberty. Making different shapes with the body helps develop an understanding of shape, space and representation. It can help develop the children's physical and verbal vocabulary as they make curved, straight, smooth, spiky, narrow, wide, twisted, stretched and arched shapes. It can also have links with writing if the children make the shapes of different letters and numbers and use their growing vocabulary to describe them.

Case study

Harrison was an early walker, taking his first steps at 10 months and walking confidently by a year. His parents encouraged him to walk when they went into town but took the pushchair along for when he got tired. They did not use reins but let him walk at his own pace and allowed him to go ahead or off sideways, just keeping a close eye on traffic. They often took the longer route through the park so that he could have more freedom to explore. He liked to go under bike racks and squeeze between lamp posts and buildings. At 19 months, Harrison liked to experiment with different ways of walking: forwards, backwards and sideways. He would beep when going backwards, like a lorry reversing. He experimented with other ways of moving too and could run, jump, spin, climb and semi-skip. By 21 months he had added shuffle, stomp, lunge and a variety of silly walks. At 28 months he could march in time to music with strong beats. As his imagination developed he would turn into a cat and prowl, gallop like a horse or bounce like a bunny. His parents allowed him to

Case study—Cont'd

bounce on their bed. At 33 months he demonstrated a variety of bounces which he named:

- Dancing bounce
- Sitting bounce
- Slop bounce
- Twist bounce
- Knee bounce
- Pointy bounce.

His older sister took gymnastics and he liked to copy her. He could do forward rolls and had his own versions of handstands and cartwheels. As he approached 3 years old, he often called, 'Look what I can do!' before demonstrating a particular physical feat, such as jumping across a mat or holding a balance.

Reflections for the early career professional

- How often do children get to move about in your setting? How often is this in a controlled, orderly way?
- What do you do to encourage children to move in different ways?

Reflections for the leader/manager

- How do you provide freedom of exploration for individuals within a group while ensuring health and safety?
- What impact does parenting or teaching style have on children's development?
- How does this range of movement relate to dance?

The space

It is important to consider the space which you provide for dance. Even an individual child dancing requires quite a lot of space in order to have the freedom to move expressively. If you have a large group of children you will probably need to go outside or use an empty hall. Very young children are still developing the concept of how much space their own body takes up which makes it difficult for them to negotiate through crowded spaces, although by around 3 years old most will have good spatial awareness and being able to manoeuvre around objects (Meggitt and Sunderland, 2000: 70). Some teachers use rubber spots on the floor to indicate the space for each child if the dance focuses on a small area rather than travelling but this clearly has limitations. As well as considering the length and breadth of the room for travelling, it is important to remember the height. Adults tend to move at one level, the aging bones feeling reluctant to bend or crouch. While dancing, you need to think about the levels and make conscious decisions about whether a move should be low, medium or high or should make transitions between these. Line dancing and country dancing both involve a range of directions, with moves going forwards, backwards and sideways. These directions should be explored in other forms of dance as well.

The quality

Exploring what the body can do and the space around them comes quite naturally to children, given the opportunity. Consciously analysing the quality of the movements requires more intervention. As discussed in the Listening section, different types of music can inspire different types of movement. Two pieces from Grieg's Peer Gynt serve as a good example. 'In the Hall of the Mountain King' with its heavy, sombre beginning, leading to a frantic, explosive climax will provoke very different movements from children then 'Morning' with its smooth, lulling, floating and swelling melody. Relating movements to music, pictures and animals will help children to explore the qualities of movement while they develop the vocabulary needed to describe them. Emotions can also help children explore the qualities of movement. Have the children walk around the space and ask them to change their walk to show that they are angry, sad, excited, tired or happy. They can take turns to watch each others' movements and then discuss what qualities made the movement fit the emotion and the fact that different children will express emotions in different ways.

The relationships

The age of the children will be a prime factor when thinking about the different groupings for dance. Babies and toddlers will dance by themselves or with their parent or carer. You might have a circle dance like 'Here we go round the Mulberry Bush' with a toddler group but only if there is a large number of adults to support the children. From 18 months they start to take more of an interest in each other and begin to interact by chasing and copying (Bee and Boyd, 2004: 310). This provides some potential for partner work, which can become more structured as they get older. Smith et al. (2003: 141) recommend using partners initially for 2–4 year olds, gradually working towards bigger groups. By the age of 4 the children should be able to take part in a circle dance in a large group with only a few adults.

The role of the teacher needs to be considered carefully. If the children are copying the teacher or following specific instructions, they will be developing their movement skills but are probably not being creative. Sabin (2002: 9) describes three teaching styles: authoritarian, directed discovery and environmental discovery. The authoritarian style is very directive and is used to teach specific movements or give instructions for traditional dances, such as the 'Circassian Circle'. The directed discovery style involves questioning by the teacher to lead the children through a sequence of learning. The example of children changing their walk for different emotions given above would fit in this style. The environmental discovery allows the greatest freedom and requires the greatest creativity from the children. The teacher provides the stimuli and allows the children freedom to explore it and make decisions. Sabin states that a combination of the three styles is needed in teaching dance. However, teachers need to be aware of which style they are using and think carefully about why they are using that style at that point.

Creating a dance

Sexton (2004) provides a sequence for creating dances. As with any physical activity the children should start with a warm-up. This is both to warm-up the body and focus the mind. The next step is Improvisation, when the children come up with a collection of movements and relates to Hall's (2002) Stage 1 – the Body. This will probably involve the directed discovery approach discussed above. The teacher can give instructions or ask questions such as, 'Show me a curved shape', followed by 'Show me a different curved shape', repeated several times, to help the children build up their repertoire. This leads into Selection where the children decide which of the movements or shapes they want to use, asking for their favourite or most interesting one. The Development step is where the other three of Hall's stages are considered, with the children thinking about where, how and with whom they are going to perform their movement or shape. Some of these decisions, for instance with whom, might be taken by the teacher, although this will reduce the children's creativity. It is also at this step that you could bring together more than one movement or shape to make a sequence. During the development, your teaching style might make a transition from directed discovery to environmental discovery. Once the dance has been created, the final steps are Performance, Appraisal and Cool down. The Performance and Appraisal steps in dance are parallel to those in music. The Cool down is an important step to stretch out the children's muscles and refocus to aid the transition to the next activity.

Sexton focused entirely on creative dance. However, you might start by teaching a traditional or other set dance in an authoritarian style and then use some of the steps or structure of that dance as the basis for the children to create their own dances. These two approaches will be discussed more in the Supporting Development section.

Creating music and dance from birth to 3 years of age

Several studies with babies have examined how they listen to music. This starts with studies in utero where it has been discovered that babies in the last trimester can become familiar with pieces of music that are played repeatedly (Papousek, 1996; Young, 2003). Postpartum there have been studies that involved the babies changing the focus of their attention when they perceived changes in the sound. It was found that they could differentiate between notes less than a semitone apart (the smallest interval in Western music), recognize melodies regardless of changes to pitch or tempo, and spot changes to rhythm, all in the same way that adults do (Trehub, 2003). This increased recognition of babies' competency has led some people into 'baby training' to push their development.

Mozart effect

In the 1990s there was a study about the effect on college students of listening to Mozart before undertaking a spatial-reasoning activity that concluded that it had a positive temporary result (Rauscher et al., 1993). This became known as the Mozart effect in the media and led to various baby training and school programmes based on using Mozart, with the promise that this would make your child more intelligent. This was not what the original study had concluded and subsequent studies have further questioned the links between listening to Mozart and performance on various intelligence measures (Crncec et al., 2006; Hui, 2006; McKelvie and Low, 2002), although there have also been studies which demonstrate that listening to Mozart seems to activate certain regions of the brain which could have a temporary benefit (Suda et al., 2008). Despite the fact that the initial study was performed on university students and has since been seriously questioned, an industry has sprouted up from this aimed at babies and young children, for example, the trade marking of the term 'Mozart Effect' and using it to sell music CDs for educational purposes. There have also been baby DVDs, combining classical music with images, which some parents buy in the expectation of increased intelligence (Slevin, 2007). There is little evidence of their educational impact and one study showed that watching baby DVDs can have a negative impact on language development when watched by babies 8–16 months (Zimmerman et al., 2007). I do not want to stop people playing Mozart, or any other music, to their children but do want to caution them against expecting this to increase their children's intelligence.

The links between sound and movement

Babies are often soothed by sounds and movements. Parents sing and automatically rock their babies (Young, 2003). We often put musical mobiles on cots. I remember long nights of dancing to Patsy Cline with an unsettled baby, willing her to go to sleep and be content. Around 1 and 2 months children begin to have more control of their heads, hands and feet. They will notice the noise of a shaker or rattle and try to locate it (Bukatko and Daehler, 2004: 215). They will try to bat at dangling toys that make noises and by 3 months will enjoy holding rattles and other musical toys (Meggitt and Sunderland, 2000: 27). Young babies have a large range of sounds, from high pitched mewlings to deep throaty sounds (Health Promotion England, 2000: 31). As they get older, 4–6 months, they may join in if you sing to them, using their own range of sounds. This experimenting with sounds and babbling will increase from around 6 months as they move towards talking (Johnston and Nahmad-Williams, 2009: 152). At 7 months, Freya discovered that she could make interesting sounds if she flapped her fist in front of her mouth while babbling. Responding to the child's vocalizations, either with praise or by echoing them, will encourage further experimentation. The 'motherese' or sing-song speech that is often adopted by adults when speaking to babies has been shown in international studies to help develop children's language development and to contribute to children's musical development (Papousek, 1996; Trehub, 2003). You can also develop the idea of taking turns in conversations, a basic musical structure, by answering the child's vocalizations or other sounds (see Callander and Nahmad-Williams, 2010). At 8 months, Pippa liked to stand and bang her hands on stools and her toy chest. She liked it even more if it turned into a banging conversation with one of her parents. From around a year, you can encourage children to experiment with volume by whispering to them. Since toddlers tend to have very loud voices it is good to demonstrate early on that it is possible to speak very quietly.

Children in the womb get to hear the steady pulse of their mother's heartbeat. As babies they respond to strong beats. In the first few months before they can crawl, jigging and trotting songs are especially popular because they reinforce the beat of the music with movement. With increasing mobility comes increased dancing. It is good to provide a variety of music with strong beats to inspire dancing but children will also dance to interesting rhythms without tunes too. At 10 months, Dominic performed a knee bending bob while standing in response to the rhythms in some jazz music. At 11 months, Hannah bounced, squealed and flapped her arms to the music at a Reggae festival. At 17 months, Freya would perform different types of dances to different music. Music with strong beats resulted in triumphal foot stomping dances. Gentler music resulted in lots of spinning. Providing a range of music and modelling different types of dancing can help extend the child's range of dance movements. Videos that show dancing can be used but an adult or another child dancing with them is a greater inspiration.

Making sounds

Many electronic toys for young children include sounds and music. Songs in mobiles and rocking chairs are designed to lull the child to sleep, while those in toys are often more energetic and designed to encourage movement and interaction with the toy. Around 4 to 8 months when babies are gaining increasing control of their arms and legs, and developing an interest in exploring objects, toys which make a noise when struck encourage the baby to attempt to repeat the action to create the sound again, starting to develop the cognitive link between cause and effect (Papalia et al., 2006: 171). This develops into more purposeful music-making if you provide sound makers that can be shaken or hit. These can be instruments designed for young children, homemade instruments such as a plastic water bottle with lentils or rice, or just ordinary things around the house.

Photograph 3.3 SoundBall (© P. Hopkins)

Case study

At 2 1/2 years Pippa created her own kitchen symphony. The baking pans were kept in a low cupboard to which she had free access. She took out most of the pans and upturned them on the floor. She used wooden spoons to try out the different sounds they made and then arranged them carefully around her, putting certain sounds together. Her dad then supplied her with some chopsticks as well. She spent the next half hour drumming on the various pans changing between the wooden spoons and the chopsticks at times. This performance was repeated several times over the next few months.

Reflection for the early career professional

- What musical activities were evident in this case study?
- How do you support the children's musical explorations?

Reflection for the leader/manager

- How and when can the children in your setting access sound sources?
- Pippa demonstrated a long attention span for this activity. What impact does self-initiated activity rather than teacher-led have on your children's attention span?

Invented songs

As well as composing instrumental pieces, toddlers often compose their own songs (Trehub, 2003). Some of these will be original tunes with babbling for lyrics. Some contain lines from known songs repeated or combined with original material. One day 7-year-old Freya made up a song to a conga rhythm and we sang it together while dancing. The following day Pippa, 23 months, made up her own song to the same rhythm. The lyrics to invented songs will often relate to everyday life. At 27 months, Pippa sang, 'I like my changing nappy all my life, all my life' while her nappy was being changed. According to Gardner (1982: 151), children begin to sing learned songs around 24–30 months, although their own 'spontaneous songs' will dominate at this age. At 29 months, Pippa was adapting known songs. A particular favourite was 'Old McDonald', which would be changed to a 'kiss kiss here' one day and a 'yawn yawn there' the next day. In their research at Project Zero in the United States, Gardner (1982: 152) found that the balance changed at 3 or 4 years old, with the spontaneous songs giving way to learned songs. With my own children I noticed that they gradually sang more learned songs from about 2 1/2 years old but they continued to invent songs as well, with our encouragement, often using fragments of known songs, adapting words or creating new words to existing tunes.

Case study

A SureStart centre held a weekly singing group for under 5s. There was a mix of ages, from babes in arms to 4 year olds who attended nursery school part-time. Some people came weekly while others just came occasionally. The leader started each session with a song that welcomed everyone, children and adults, by name. She also tried to involve all of the children at different times by giving them toys that went with the song to hold or instruments to play. She used these opportunities to work on social development, focusing on taking turns, saying thank you and helping to put things away. Holly, 3 years old, was very confident. She joined in with all the songs and the actions and could remember the words. Mikhail, also 3 years old, and Raphael, 18 months, both had English as a second language. Mikhail was able to join in some of the words and usually joined in the actions. Raphael often wandered about the room but was eager to join in if a toy or instrument was on offer. Emma, 13 months, was confident about moving around the room and interacting with the adults. She did not join in with the singing but after a few weeks joined in with the actions, and like Raphael was keen to hold a toy or play an instrument. Miguel, also 13 months, came from a dual language household. He was less confident than Emma, staying close to his mother throughout the session. He would copy some actions but would not always accept toys or instruments. Maria, 4 years old, had recently arrived from Portugal. She listened carefully and joined in with the actions. Sophie, Katie and Annabel, who were all under a year and could not crawl or walk yet, seemed to listen to the singing. They would happily chew on toys or wave them about. With their parents' help they would play the instruments. The wrist bells were very popular because the children could use them without assistance. When the group sang 'Row, row, row your boat' parents were encouraged to turn their children to face them so that they could 'row' forwards and backwards while singing. Mikhail went to the leader and rowed with her, while Raphael stayed with his mother. Most of the other children were happy to be rocked back and forth by their parents, smiling and giggling. Only Holly and Mikhail were able to sing the words. Emma would not face her mother or join in the rowing but did enjoy the extra verses, screaming at the crocodile and then laughing. All of the children seemed to enjoy the parachute games with some of the songs. The babies gripped the parachute and waved it with a lot of support from their parents, the older ones held it independently and stretched high to make dramatic ups and downs. Raphael would run around and under the parachute, sometimes leaping on top of it. Other songs were accompanied by marching around the room. Those who could not yet walk were carried. The early walkers would march on their own at times but could not maintain it for the whole song. The older children marched confidently, often overtaking some of the younger ones. The session usually ended with everyone dancing the Hokey Cokey in a circle.

Reflection for the early career professional

- Do you think that the younger children benefit from this session?
- How are these activities contributing to the development of music and dance?
- How would you react to children like Raphael who wander about during the session?
- What observations can you make from this session and how would this impact on your planning for the next session?

Reflection for the leader/manager

- What are the advantages and disadvantages of having such a wide mix of ages? How does this impact on planning the session?
- How do these sessions contribute to the children's global development?
- What opportunities do the children have to be creative in this session?

Creating music and dance from 3 to 5 years of age

There are many developments that occur in this age group which have a major impact on music and dance. Physical development underwent dramatic changes from birth to 3 and it continues to make great strides between 3 and 5 as the children become increasingly confident and skilful movers. Some children will have learned to jump before 3 years old but this ability will improve, jumping higher and farther, and the children will learn to hop, gallop and skip (Bukatko and Daehler, 2004: 161). Their sense of balance improves and they become able to run on tiptoe (Meggitt and Sunderland, 2000: 78). They become more aware of how they fit into spaces, can follow a given pathway and manoeuvre around obstacles (Meggitt and Sunderland, 2000: 70, 78). These key physical developments mean that children have mastered most of the physical skills needed for dance. Duffy (2006: 107) has devised a development sequence for dance (Table 3.1) which builds on these skills.

Table 3.1 Duffy's developmental sequence for dance

3–4 years	Start to experiment with different body movements in response to music
	Enjoy exploring and practicing movements for its own sake
	March in time to music and walks on tiptoes
	Can switch from one movement to another during dance
4–5 years	Are able to master a wider range of movements, for example, skips, hops and forward jumps
	Move with increased awareness of rhythm
	Are able to use movement to interpret music, for example, will respond to 'sad' music
	Perform simple dance steps

(Duffy, 2006: 107)

Another area of change during this period is social development. As toddlers, the children will have begun to take more notice of each other and have started to interact. From around 14 to 18 months children will often engage in parallel play, begin to copy each other towards the end of that period. However, by the time they reach 3 or 4 years old the children will prefer playing with another child rather than by themselves, although there will still be periods of solitary and parallel play. This play with other children becomes increasingly imaginative and dramatic during this period, with the children taking on various roles (Bee and Boyd, 2004: 310; Smith et al., 2003: 141; Megitt and Sunderland, 2000: 81, 88). In the Introduction, music and dance were put forward as primarily social and group activities, although both can be engaged in privately and alone. These developments in children's social interactions mean that the children are more interested in engaging in music and dance as a group, considering each other's performance and responding to them.

The final aspect to consider is language development. Most children will move into using sentences during this period, with an increasing grasp of grammatical forms. Their improved language skills have an impact on their social skills because they are more able to communicate with other adults and children, understanding more and being understood (Bee and Boyd, 2004: 453, 454). Their increased language skills also relates to an increased interest in singing songs and nursery rhymes, remembering a growing repertoire (Meggitt and Sunderland, 2000: 72).

The EYFS statements for 3–5 (2008: 112) can be split into two different aspects (Table 3.2), with some statements containing both aspects: learning or

Table 3.2 Copying or Creating?

	Copying others	Creating own
30–50 months	Enjoy joining in with dancing and ring games	Explore and learn how sounds can be changed
	Sing a few familiar songs	Sing to themselves and make up simple songs
	Tap out simple repeated rhythms . . .	. . . and make some up
	Imitate . . .	. . . and create movement in response to music
40–60 + months	Begin to build a repertoire of songs and dances	Explore different sounds of instruments
	Begin to move rhythmically	

(compiled from DCSF, 2008: 112)

copying existing music and dance versus creating their own music and dance.

There is only one Early Learning Goal for this section: 'Recognise and explore how sounds can be changed, sing simple songs from memory, recognise repeated sounds and sound patterns and match movements to music' (DCSF, 2008: 112). This again has a combination of learning an existing repertoire and creating new. However, the Early Learning Goals for all of the other sections of Creative Development, 'respond in a variety of ways . . .', 'express and communicate their ideas, thoughts and feelings . . .' (DCSF, 2008: 107), 'explore . . .' (DCSF, 2008: 110) and 'use their imagination . . .' (DCSF, 2008: 114) also relate to music and dance, so this section should not be seen in isolation.

I find it interesting that the music and dance section of *Creative Development* is the only one that has an emphasis on learning the existing repertoire; the others focus, almost exclusively, on the children exploring and creating their own works. This may relate to the fact that music and dance often happen in groups, although the same is true of drama. It may also be about how these aspects are carried out in the adult world. Copying art is called forgery but copying existing pieces of music and dance is the norm for public performance. It may also be due to the fact that traditional songs and dances are important cultural artefacts and learning these is part of children's enculturation and developing identity. Nevertheless, it is vital that teachers of this age-phase ensure that children have opportunities to create their own music and dance.

Practical tasks

Review your teaching of music and dance. What is the balance between children copying, learning and performing existing music and dance versus creating their own? How do the opportunities for free play in music and dance compare to those in art and role-play?

Resources

Providing inspiring resources can help release the children's creativity. Good quality instruments can be purchased, including some designed specifically for young children. Make sure that the instruments play properly as well as look and feel attractive, since some companies produce instruments as 'toys' and do not pay sufficient attention to the sound production. This is particularly true of children's xylophones, glockenspiels and recorders, which frequently are not tuned to a Western scale. Children will enjoy making their own instruments but these should supplement rather than replace a professional collection. However, it is good to include some everyday objects as sound sources as well, building on children's earlier experiences of exploring sound in the home. One of the most interesting 'instruments' I had in school was a metal amaretti biscuit tin. The sides were corrugated, the bottom was smooth metal and the lid was plastic with several raised concentric circles. It could be struck or scraped, making different sounds on each surface. Add some rice inside and it could also be shaken. Children at this age should be exploring the sound potential of instruments, and doing this with everyday objects helps them to see the many possibilities there are. Your instrument collection could include the following:

- Maracas and other shakers
- Rainsticks
- Tambourines
- Tambours
- Large gathering drum with large beaters
- Bells on sticks and bracelets/anklets
- Triangles of different sizes

- Indian bells, cymbals
- Agogos and wood blocks for striking
- Guiros and frogs for scraping
- Tuned percussion: Xylophones, glockenspiels, chime bars, hand bells.

The instruments can be used to accompany singing, for composing and performing instrumental pieces and as the basis for movement. You can also use recorded music, although Davies (2003: 165) cautions that recording music should be used 'sparingly' with children 2–4 years old because they find it hard to match their movements to someone else's complex rhythms and patterns. However, my experience is that recorded music can create strong urges in children to dance, whether they attend to its particular patterns or not. Some of the music that resulted in Pippa leaping up to dance, and demanding we joined her, were the 'Sleeping Beauty' ballet, 'Come on Eileen' by Dexys Midnight Runners, 'Thank God I'm a Country Boy' by John Denver, 'Awu Wemadoda' by Ladysmith Black Mombazo and 'In the Mood' by Glen Miller. I would recommend playing a range of music, including different styles, countries and times.

A variety of dressing up clothes will lead to different sorts of dance:

- Tutus – ballet
- Full skirts/dresses – spinning
- Pirate outfits – swashbuckling
- Soldier outfits – marching
- Superhero capes – leaping
- Wizard/witch – arm waving
- Cowboy/cowgirl – energetic
- Clown outfit – silly, exaggerated movements
- King/queen – stately

Clothing from different parts of the world will help children to explore the dance of different cultures because the type and cut of the fabric impact on the movements that can be performed.

- Sari
- Flamenco dress
- Hula skirt
- Chinese dragon mask and cape
- Kilt

Simple props like balls, skipping ropes, hoops, rubber spots and lines for the floor can also aid the imagination. Long pieces of cloth, scarves and ribbon sticks will encourage large, graceful, flowing movements.

Photograph 3.4 Wings (© P. Hopkins)

Case study

The nursery children come into the classroom gradually with their parents. The parents stay for about 10 minutes and help the children settle in by doing an activity with them. To help make the transition from entering with their parents to large-group time, the nursery class spend 15 minutes in front of the whiteboard following the instructions and copying the actions of the virtual teacher in the video. They warm-up with stretches and fast movements. This progresses to different movements to music and movements to match different images. Helen, the class teacher, stands at the side and participates along with the class. She encourages the children to participate and comments on individuals who are moving particularly well or are especially focused.

Reflection for the early career professional

- What are the advantages and disadvantages of having a virtual teacher?
- What are the advantages and disadvantages of having frequent short movement sessions?

Reflection for the leader/manager

- How does this sort of activity fit into a creative dance programme?
- How do routines like these contribute to the overall structure of the session?

Performance issues

At this age parents and teachers will often hear children calling 'Look at me!' or 'Watch this!' as they perform some new feat. This urge to perform can be beneficial in music and dance but there is no guarantee that the children will want to perform on demand. Some children will be motivated by a special performance place, such as a raised platform, while others will find this off-putting. Several schools I work in have installed raised wooden platforms in the playground. These are used extensively at playtime with the children performing impromptu songs, dances and dramas for themselves. When Freya was 3 1/2 years we were in a dining hall that had a raised area at one end. She decided that it was a stage and proceeded to perform several songs and dances. The fact that nobody was watching was immaterial because it was the performance itself that was important to her rather than the presence of an audience. I recommend sensitively encouraging the children to perform by providing them with choices about what they perform, where, when and to whom. They might just want to perform for another child or their mother. However, I also recommend extensive use of ICT, such as video cameras, tape recorders and digital cameras, to record both works-in-progress and performances. OfSTED (2009: 18) noted that recordings were not being used enough in schools for assessment. The children should review the recordings in order to self-assess their own work, identifying what they liked and what they want to improve. This is also helpful for the teacher's assessments and record keeping. I used to make assessment notes while the children were creating and practicing, while they performed and again as they responded to the recording. Towards the end of the year the children liked to watch/listen to the recordings again, which led to fruitful discussions about how much progress had been made during the year.

Transition to Key Stage 1 (5 to 7 years of age)

In the EYFS, dance comes under the heading of Creative Development. In the National Curriculum dance is a subsection of Physical Education. This could represent a philosophical change from an emphasis on creativity to an emphasis on skills. However, children in Key Stage 1 are still required to make decisions about dance, combining movements, exploring space and changing levels so creativity should still be evident in good dance sessions. Nevertheless, the move to Key Stage 1 has other implications for children's dance opportunities. The Key Stage 1 Physical Education (PE) curriculum includes dance, gymnastics and games, but may also include additional aspects such as swimming. Since dance is only one third of PE at most, which is only one of eleven or more curriculum subjects, it clearly will receive limited time and emphasis. As part of PE, dance will usually be taught in a specific timetabled session, usually in the school hall, with the whole class together. This leads to a very teacher-directed approach and makes spontaneous, individual, child-led dance unlikely.

Music is a separate foundation subject in the National Curriculum and so is likely to receive greater time than dance at Key Stage 1. In some schools it is taught in the hall or in a special music room but frequently it takes place in the classroom, which means that there is more flexibility in when and for how long it is taught. However, it is still likely to be a timetabled, teacher-directed lesson rather than spontaneous and child-led. Some classes set out a music corner with instruments where children can initiate their own music but there are often concerns about the other children being disrupted so these are not used as fully or as spontaneously as they might be. Custodero (2005) noted with concern the reduction in opportunities for children to initiate their own musical activities as they got older. This emphasis on teacher-led activities in music and dance can result in the teacher's creativity taking precedence over the children's creativity. Nevertheless, creativity is a requirement of both music and dance at Key Stage 1, made explicit in such statements as: '2a create musical patterns'; '3a explore and express their ideas and feelings about music using movement, dance and expressive and musical language' (DfEE, 1999: 124); '6a use movement imaginatively, responding to stimuli, including music, and performing basic skills'; '6c create and perform dances using simple movement patterns, including those from different times and cultures' (DfEE, 1999: 131). Some of these statements also reinforce the connection between music and dance that is present in the Foundation Stage.

Practical tasks

Plan some opportunities for child initiated and led music and dance. Consider the organizational implications including time, space, resources, noise/disruption to others. Are these significantly different in the Foundation Stage and Key Stage 1?

Observe how children take up these opportunities. Are there differences in their achievement between child-initiated and teacher-led activities?

Supporting the development of music and dance

Too often activities that are labelled as creative in schools, nurseries and at home are about filling time, learning a set of techniques or decoration rather than being truly creative, intellectual activities. Pre-printed, adult-directed and mass-produced art work does not lead to creativity. The images that children create using these methods are not their own. Such work may occupy children and fill empty walls. It may look pretty and be admired, but it will not encourage imagination and creativity.

(Duffy, 2006: 11)

Although Duffy's example refers to art, the same principle applies to music and dance. It is important to remember that this area of learning is creative development so there needs to be an emphasis on developing creativity in all of the activities. If the children are singing a song that you have taught them as a whole class, are they being creative? The same question can apply to the performance of a structured dance that you have taught them. In both cases the answer is that it depends. Individual creativity depends on the individual making choices; however, you can also be creative as a group. Nevertheless, the children must be involved in making the choices if their creativity is to be developed rather than just the teacher's.

Supporting invented song

As stated earlier, young children will create their own music while singing; however, this becomes less common as they get older and begin to perceive composition as belonging only to professional musicians. In order to nurture their early-compositional abilities, it is important that the adults value the songs that they make. This can be done by praising the songs, commenting on aspects you particularly enjoyed. Some children will enjoy the opportunity to perform their songs for others. I taught a boy in Year 1 who frequently asked if he could perform his new song for the class at the beginning of the day. An important way to encourage this sort of composition is modelling. You can do this by singing your own invented songs. This can work very well as a behaviour-management technique. Quietly singing 'Which table is ready to go, ready to go, ready to go? Which table is ready to go? All are tidy and quiet' is effective at getting the children's attention without having to raise your voice and focuses them on the desired behaviour. Using a familiar tune and repeated phrases you can come up with little songs to match many occasions. Although singing is a very natural human activity, many adults are scared and self-conscious about singing. You act as a role model for the children so it is important that you project a positive attitude. It helps to remember that children are much less critical as an audience than adults. If you are very worried about your singing ability you can always chant or rap.

Finding the singing voice

As well as encouraging children's composition, you need to help children develop their singing voice. Although some children learn how to sing in tune at an early age, usually having experienced a musical environment, many children 'are unaware of their singing voice and have to be shown how to find it' (Pearce, 1998: 26). Children who have not yet found their singing voice resort to 'rhythmic talking or monotoning on a low note' (Pearce, 1998: 26). One way of helping children find their singing voice is by sliding. The leader (an adult or child) raises and lowers hands and the singers follow this by sliding their voices higher and lower on a vowel sound to whatever pitches they feel comfortable with. You can make this more interesting by using the sounds to create different atmospheres. An 'oo' sound is ghostly, an 'ah' sound is floaty, while 'ee' or a mixture of vowels can be alien. Another activity to help find the voice is to use different pitches for different characters in stories, such as a deep, gruff voice for daddy bear, a sweet, medium pitched voice for mummy bear and a high, sad voice for baby bear.

Proper breath support is vital to singing well. This has implications for classroom organization. It is extremely difficult to breathe properly while sitting cross-legged on the floor. Kneeling is better for breath support but bad for circulation. If the children are sitting on the floor, make sure that they stand up to sing some of the time. It is much better to be sitting on a bench or chair. However, posture is important here too. The children should sit forward on the chair, not leaning against the back, and feet should be flat on the floor. Legs should not be crossed as this inhibits your diaphragm and reduces control of the lungs. Remember that it is important for you to model good posture when singing. OfSTED (2009: 9) found that where singing was a strength, the pupils were taught about posture, breathing and how to use a singing voice from the Foundation Stage.

Singing in groups, especially with mixed ages, can help children find their voice. Children are better at matching their voices to another voice rather than to an instrument; so accompaniment is best kept to a minimum when first singing. If they are not used to hearing a male voice some children will have initial difficulties matching their pitch to a man's which may be one or two octaves lower. Using falsetto can help, but the children will adjust fairly quickly if they hear the male voice regularly. If you are still struggling to find your own singing voice you could use recorded music to sing with but it is important that you sing along as well so that you can act as a positive role model and so that you can work on developing your own skills.

Unfortunately, I have encountered many adults who were told as children that they could not sing. This can have a devastating and long-lasting effect. Some children will take longer to find their singing voice than others and will require differentiated support. It is important that you encourage these children and recognize what they can do. Putting an uncertain singer with strong singers will help provide support. Large groups also provide support but make it difficult to hear the individual voices. Do not put children on the spot to sing a solo and never use solo singing as a threat.

Case study

James at 10 years old enjoyed singing and joined the school choir but still had not found his singing voice and was at the same level as many 4-year-olds. He could sing rhythmically but stayed on the same one or two low notes. He struggled to match pitches and could not imitate the contours of the tune. In the choir sessions I used my hands to show the shape of the tune and had the children copy the movements as they sang. I used the Orff technique of echoing and improvising, combining singing and playing tuned percussion (xylophones, metallophones, glockenspiels and chime bars), initially using just two notes that were in the range James was comfortable with and gradually extending both the range and the number of notes. Progress was slow but after several months James was able to sing in tune with the rest of the choir, although he was still uncertain when singing alone.

Reflection for the early career professional

- How do you differentiate in music and dance for those who need more support and those who need extending?
- Find out more about Orff Schulwerk (see recommended reading). Would this approach fit into your music curriculum?

Reflection for the leader/manager

- What is your view about differentiation in the arts subjects? How does this impact on practice?
- Find out more about Orff Schulwerk and Dalcroze Eurythmics (see recommended reading). How do these approaches relate to your philosophy about music and movement education?

Choosing appropriate songs is an important way of supporting children's singing. The first songs should have melodies that move in steps rather than leaping about and have a fairly small range, pitched in the middle of the voice. 'Mary had a little lamb' fits these criteria particularly well, whereas 'Boys and girls come out to play' has a large range, from low notes to high notes, and is difficult for young children to sing well. The following list includes some nursery rhymes that are easy to sing:

- Baa, baa black sheep
- Twinkle, twinkle, little star
- Mary, Mary quite contrary
- The grand old duke of York
- Polly put the kettle on
- One, two buckle my shoe
- 1 2 3 4 5, once I caught a fish alive
- Hey diddle diddle
- Pat a cake
- Pease pudding hot
- Row, row, row your boat
- Teddy bear, teddy bear
- Frere Jacques
- Incy wincy spider
- Do you know the muffin man?

Creative dance

In order to create dance, there needs to be a starting point or initial idea. This could be the music itself (as described in several examples previously) or it could be a drawing, photograph, statue, story, poem, situation or topic. These provide opportunities to make cross-curricular links with other aspects of the children's learning.

Swindlehurst and Chapman (2008) recommend the use of action words to develop creative dance. The teacher and/or children come up with a list of action words related to a theme. For example, for the theme 'Spring' you might have words like grow, stretch, shine, drip, build, open, melt. These words are combined into movement phrases and gradually develop into a dance.

One of the teacher's roles is to help the children stylize their movements, by thinking about the qualities and whether to move quickly or slowly, smoothly or sharply, strong or delicate etc. Sexton (2004: 33–35) recommends helping the children develop their movements into sequences by getting them to experiment with changes. For instance:

- Change the speed
- Change the level
- Make the movement bigger

- Make the movement smaller
- Make the movement on a different body part
- Add another movement
- Repeat part of the movement
- Remove part of the movement

This type of exploration will result in a more stylized form, helping to make the transition from movement into dance. Throughout this process keep focusing the children on the various aspects of dance (described in several sets of four earlier in the chapter) and get them to make decisions based on these. The structure of the dance, especially how it will begin and end, is something with which young children need considerable support. If this support is given through questioning rather than suggestions it helps to ensure that the creative decisions belong to the children rather than the teacher.

Traditional dance

The other aspect of dance in the early-years curriculum is learning existing dances. This can begin with very simple dances such as 'Ring a ring o' roses' or 'In and out the dusty bluebells'. In Nursery and Reception this can extend to traditional folk dances, such as English and Scottish country dancing. I would recommend using country dances that are based on a ring because it means all the children share a common focus and the teacher can easily watch and support the whole group. A modified Circassian circle can be danced success-fully by young children. For example,

- All hold hands in a circle, with bands on every other child.
- All walk forwards for four and backwards for four. Repeat.
- Banded children walk forward for four (and clap) and backwards for four (and clap).
- Unbanded children walk forward for four (and clap) and backwards for four (and clap).
- All join hands in the circle again. Walk the circle anticlockwise for 16 and then clockwise for 16, ready to start again.

As the children become confident with this you can make it more challenging by skipping rather than walking in the circle. The next step would be to get banded and unbanded partners to turn together for 16 beats and omit circling clockwise. For the full version of the Circassian circle the final change would be to have the partners promenade together anticlockwise rather than the whole circle holding hands at that point. With older children and adults this is developed further by having the partners split and progress to a new partner as they reform the circle to start again. If you feel the first version of the dance was still too challenging for your children you could simplify it further by keeping the children together at all times so the whole circle goes forward and backwards twice or four times before circling.

I have suggested banded and unbanded, rather than boys and girls, as a way to identify the dancers. Young children are quite happy to dance with their own gender. Forcing mixed gender partnerships can cause some children to feel uncomfortable and will cause problems if you have unequal numbers of boys and girls. You can just number the children 1, 2 around the circle but unless you have a way of identifying them visually you are likely to have difficulties because many of the children will forget the number they were assigned.

Once the children have learned some traditional dances these can serve as the basis for children to create their own in the same style. The improvisation stage would involve analysing and practicing the steps that make up the dances they have learned. The teacher might also teach them some additional steps, such as clapping own hands and then clapping with the partner. The selection stage would be when the class decided which moves to include. The development stage would require decisions about how the moves were put together into the dance sequence. This process allows you to address both the imitative and creative aspects of the dance curriculum.

Planning for music and dance

How much time?

A pupil talking to an OfSTED inspector about amount of music teaching said: 'It depends on the teacher. My teacher this year really likes music and we do a lot but last year we hardly did any; there was always something else we had to do first' (OfSTED, 2009: 20).

Although this pupil was being interviewed about music, in my experience the same is true about all the aspects of creative development. I was that teacher who enjoyed music and dance and so ensured that it happened. One year I was able to have double dance sessions for most of a term because the teacher who had the hall after me was one of those who found something else to do instead of dance and so would come into the hall late or not at all. Unfortunately, this type of situation means that children's entitlement to a broad and balanced curriculum is at risk.

Cross-curricular planning can help provide more time through the integration of several areas of learning. The EYFS (2008) encourages a cross-curricular approach that helps children to make connections. After a subject dominated approach through the 1990s, the primary curriculum has been moving towards a more cross-curricular approach, encouraged first by *Excellence and Enjoyment* (2003) and more recently by the *Rose Review* (2009). As was stated in the Introduction, music and dance have been part of cultures around the world, across religions and throughout time. This means that they can link easily to topics about Time, Place or Communities. Both music and dance can be used to explore scientific ideas such as growth, change, forces and the variety in living things. If you cannot find a song to match your topic you can always take an existing tune and write new words for it, as done by Nicholls (2004) in the *Handy Band*. There are strong links between mathematics and music and dance, with number, pattern, shape and space featuring heavily. There are many obvious relationships between singing and literacy. However, OfSTED (2009: 20) warned that when cross-curricular links were made with music ' . . . the emphasis given to literacy and other subjects often overshadowed the musical learning that might have taken place.' You need to be very clear when you are planning and assessing whether the music/dance is the main focus of the lesson, an equal focus with other areas of learning or merely a tool to aid learning in the other area.

Case study

A primary school was having a special week based around Religious Education but using a cross-curricular approach. One aspect of this was a performance by the whole school about the Christian story of Creation. A group of teacher-training students worked with the different classes, with each year group taking on a different day in the story. The children worked with the students to compose music and create a dance or movement for their day. The Reception class made simple composition choices. The students had rewritten the words of 'Old McDonald' to 'God created all the world, praise oh praise his name'. The children chose different

⇨

animals for each verse and the noises and actions that would go with them. They then explored the ways the different animals moved and each child decided which animal to be and how to move. The Year 1 class split into two groups. One group used instruments to represent the land while the other used instruments to represent the sea. They used their voices and movement to represent the growth of different plants once the sea and the land were separated. The Year 2 class was split into several small groups. Each group was given a picture of a sea creature or bird and then used voices or instruments to compose music to match their animal. The class then decided how to put the various groups together, deciding on overlapping some of them and having some linking music to connect the different parts. The dance explored the different ways that the animals moved in the sea and in the air, but also the similarities. The students had composed a three part choral response to be sung between each 'day' and taught different parts to different classes. At the end of the week the school came together and performed.

Reflection for the early career professional

- When including music and dance in a cross-curricular topic how do you ensure that the specific music and dance skills are taught and assessed?
- Examine your planning for the next few weeks. Are there opportunities to integrate music and dance into other aspects of learning?

Reflection for the leader/manager

- What are the advantages and disadvantages of special events like an Arts Week or a school performance?
- How much creativity is required by the staff to provide opportunities for the children to be creative in music and dance?

Who teaches music and dance?

In the Early Years and Key Stage 1 in England and Wales, one teacher usually teaches all areas of learning or subjects. However, there is evidence (Wilson, 2008; Russell-Bowie, 2008; Swindlehurst and Chapman, 2008) that some teachers lack confidence in teaching arts subjects because they perceive them as having technical demands beyond their skills and knowledge. This has resulted in some schools using specialist arts teachers for these subjects. OfSTED (2009) found that specialist teachers were usually better at teaching music, although they also noted that some outstanding music lessons were taught by generalist class teachers. The Music Manifesto (2006: 14) recommended that early-years workers should have more professional development in music so that they could become more confident in teaching it. For several years I was involved with the Schools Music Association, helping provide music courses for generalist teachers. Although we did get some generalist teachers, we had a higher proportion of teachers who were already confident in music, wanting to extend their skills. This matches one of the findings of Wilson et al. (2008); headteachers reported that some teachers who acknowledged that they lacked skills in teaching the arts were still unwilling to go on courses to develop these skills. However, Swindlehurst and Chapman (2008) reported a high demand for courses on teaching dance. Craft (2002: 171) states that teachers need both personal and professional development as 'nourishment' to help them teach creatively and teach for creativity.

The Music Manifesto also recommended that skilled musicians should lead music sessions with children under 5 (Music Manifesto, 2006: 42). I have some worries about this approach. It confirms the teachers' beliefs that specialist skills are needed to teach the arts and it conveys this message to the children as well. They may think that if their teacher is not able to do music then maybe they do not have the necessary skills either. This then perpetuates the problem. I would like to see class teachers teaching the arts, occasionally supported by professional artists. Those who are particularly lacking in confidence could team-teach until they felt sufficiently confident to teach alone.

Practical tasks

Examine your own confidence levels in teaching music and dance. What training and past experiences of music and dance do you have? Make lists of the aspects in which you do and do not feel confident. What sort of INSET or support do you need to increase your confidence?

Home support for music and dance

The involvement of parents and carers is an important factor in all aspects of development, including music and dance (DCSF, 2008; McPherson, 2009;

Music Manifesto, 2006). McPherson (2009) found that parents' attitudes towards music and beliefs about musical ability had an impact on their children's perseverance in learning music. To support children in music and dance, parents need to value these activities and believe that their children are capable of achieving in them. One way of demonstrating value is to provide opportunities for children to engage in music and dance in the home and in the community.

Nursery rhymes and traditional songs

OfSTED's report, *Making More of Music* (2009: 10) included a statement from a Foundation Stage teacher that there has been a reduction in the number of children who entered school already familiar with traditional nursery rhymes, songs and games. I asked a group of mothers of toddlers about the nursery rhymes they sang with their children. The majority did sing some nursery rhymes but many said that the children had learned the nursery rhymes at a play group or nursery because the mothers did not know many themselves. However, there are ways of overcoming this barrier with the use of ICT. Some mothers used tapes or CDs of nursery rhymes, especially during car journeys, to teach both themselves and their children. Others had learned songs from watching children's television programmes or DVDs. Recently when I could not remember the tune to a song I looked it up on the internet and was able to play several recordings of it. My 2-year-old daughter loves watching nursery rhymes on YouTube and singing along. Nurseries and schools can help parents and carers by inviting them to singing sessions with their children. They can also make recordings of the children singing. Digital recordings can be put on the school's VLE so that parents and carers can learn them and sing them with their children, while tape recordings could be sent home, perhaps in a story sack with a relevant book and toys.

The EYFS principle Parents as Partners (DCSF, 2008) emphasizes that there should be a 'two-way flow of information, knowledge and expertise between parents and practitioners'. Some parents and carers already know a wealth of nursery rhymes and traditional songs. You could invite them in to teach some songs to you and the children and make recordings of these. If some of the parents come from other cultures or speak different languages this can be a way of building up a multicultural song bank. Demonstrating in this way that you value other cultures contributes to the EYFS principles of Inclusive Practice and the Wider Context (DCSF, 2008).

Music, dance and Islam

According to the Muslim Council of Britain (MCB) (2007), within Islam there is a range of opinions about music, based on different interpretations of the religion and their culture, which may result in some Muslim families wanting to exclude their children from music lessons. However, there is a rich tradition of Islamic music and incorporating some of these songs into your lessons may overcome reluctance from the families. Traditional Islamic music is vocal, accompanied only by untuned percussion (MCB, 2007: 52). This is actually beneficial when singing with young children because they find it easier to match their pitch to a human voice rather than a tuned instrument. Also, the lack of tuned accompaniment means that the children's voices will not be drowned out.

Dance can also be an issue for Muslim families, especially if it involves physical contact between genders and if it is performed before an audience (MCB, 2007). In my experience prepubescent children prefer dancing with members of the same gender so this could be a way forward. However, the MCB's (2007: 39) description of dance as 'expressive and creative movements connected with emotions and forces of nature' involving young children would be acceptable to most Muslims. Billingham (2007) recommends calling it movement rather than dance and emphasizing the educational aspects of movement and music lessons, rather than the 'fun' aspects. Since some families may have problems with music being used to accompany dance, Billingham (2007) notes that some schools have used natural world sounds, such as wind, sea, animal noises, to accompany their movement. Alternatively, you could use untuned percussion. There are traditional Islamic dances which could be part of the movement sessions as well.

Practical tasks

Review the music and dance materials you have used recently and examine them for inclusion issues. How do you take into account the interests or requirements of different groups? Do you think about gender, stage of development, cultural background, religion, personal interests? Do you make links between school and the music and dance of the home?

Conclusion

Music and dance are both integral parts of children's development from birth and even before. Children explore these areas naturally but a skilful adult can deepen these experiences through providing opportunities and encouragement, a rich environment, appropriate resources, stimulating questions and inspiring models. It must always be at the forefront of thought that this area is called Creating Music and Dance and is part of Creative Development so we must ensure that children have opportunities to create their own music and dance and not only perform the music and dance of others.

References

Bee, H. and Boyd, D. (2004) *The Developing Child.* 10th Edition. New York: Pearson

Billingham, C. (ed.) (2007) *Responding to School-Based Issues: Islam.* Leicester: Leicester City Council

Bukatko, D. and Daehler, M. (2004) *Child Development.* 5th Edition. Boston, MA: Houghton Mifflin

Callander, N. and Nahmad-Williams, L. (2010) *Communication, Language and Literacy.* London: Continuum

Compton, A. (1999) 'Children's Musical Listening Preferences'. Unpublished thesis, Hull: University of Hull

Craft, A. (2002) *Creativity and Early Years Education.* London: Continuum

Crncec, R., Wilson, S. and Prior, M. (2006) 'The Cognitive and Academic Benefits of Music to Children: Facts and Fiction', *Educational Psychology*, Vol. 26, No. 4: 579–594

Custadero, L. (2005) 'Musical Engagement in Young Children', *Music Education Research*, Vol. 7, No. 2: 185–209

Davies, M. (2003) *Movement and Dance in Early Childhood.* London: Sage

DCSF (2008) *The Early Years Foundation Stage; Setting the standard for learning, development and care for children from birth to five; Practice Guidance.* London: DCSF

DfEE/QCA (1999) *Music – The National Curriculum for England.* London: DfEE/QCA

DfES (2003) *Excellence and Enjoyment.* London: DfES

Duffy, B. (2006) *Supporting Creativity and Imagination in the Early Years.* 2nd Edition. Buckingham: Open University Press

Gardner, H. (1982) *Art, Mind and Brain.* New York: Basic Books

Hall, J. (2002) *Dance for Infants.* 2nd Edition. London: A and C Black

Health Promotion England (2000) *Birth to Five.* London: Health Promotion England

Hui, K. (2006) 'Mozart Effect in Preschool Children?', *Early Child Development and Care*, Vol. 176, Nos. 3–4: 411–419

Johnston, J. and Nahmad-Williams, L. (2009) *Early Childhood Studies.* Harlow: Pearson Education Ltd

Lipscomb, B. (2000) *Primrose Dance Lessons for Physical Education in the Primary School.* Lancaster: Primrose Education Resources

McKelvie, P. and Low, J. (2002) 'Listening to Mozart Does Not Improve Children's Spatial Ability: Final Curtains for the Mozart Effect', *British Journal of Developmental Psychology*, Vol. 20, No. 2: 241–258

McPherson, G. (2009) 'The role of parents in children's musical development', *Psychology of Music*, Vol. 37, No. 1: 91–110

Meggitt, C. and Sunderland, G. (2000) *Child Development: An Illustrated Guide.* Oxford: Heinemann

Music Manifesto (2006) *Making Every Child's Music Matter: Music Manifesto Report No. 2.* London: Music Manifesto

Muslim Council of Britain (MCB) (2007) *Towards Greater Understanding: Meeting the Needs of Muslim Pupils in State Schools.* London: MCB

Nicholls, S. (2004) *The Handy Band: Supporting Personal, Social and Emotional Development with New Songs from Old Favourites.* London: A and C Black

Ofsted (2009) *Making More of Music.* London: Ofsted

Papalia, D., Olds, S. and Feldman, R. (2006) *A Child's World.* 10th Edition. New York: McGraw Hill

Papousek, M. (1996) 'Intuitive Parenting: A Hidden Source of Musical Stimulation in Infancy'. In Deliege, I. and Sloboda, J. (eds) *Musical Beginning: Origins and Development of Musical Competence.* Oxford: Oxford University Press, 88–99

Pearce, G. (1998) 'Developing Children's Singing', *Music in the Curriculum*, Vol. 37: 26–28

Rauscher, F., Shaw, G. and Ky, K. (1993) 'Music and Spatial Task Performance', *Nature*, Vol. 365, 611

Rose, J. (2009) *Independent Review of the Primary Curriculum: Final Report.* Nottingham: DCSF

Russell-Bowie, D. (2008) 'Perceptions of Confidence and Background in the Arts of Preservice Primary Teachers from Five Countries'. Paper Presented at the British Educational Research Association Annual Conference, Heriot-Watt University, Edinburgh, 5 September 2008

Sabin, V. (2002) *Primary School Dance: Reception and Key Stage 1.* Northampton: Val Sabin Publications

Sexton, K. (2004) *The Dance Teacher's Survival Guide.* Alton: Dance Books

Slevin, C. (2007) 'Baby Einstein Founder Stands behind Her Videos', *The Seattle Times*, 18 August 2007 [on-line www.seattletimes.nwsource.com/html/localnews/2003842093_babyeinstein18m.html]

Smith, P., Cowie, H. and Blades, M. (2003) *Understanding Children's Development.* 4th Edition. Oxford: Blackwell

Suda, M., Morimoto, K., Obata, A., Koizumi, H. and Maki, A. (2008) 'Cortical Responses to Mozrt's Sonata Enhance Spatial-Reasoning Ability', *Neurological Research*, Vol. 30, No. 9: 885–888

Swindlehurst, G. and Chapman, A. (2008) 'Teaching Dance a Framework for Creativity'. In Lavin, J. (ed.) *Creative Approaches to Physical Education.* Abingdon: Routledge, 29–54

Trehub, S. (2003) 'The Developmental Origins of Musicality', *Nature Neuroscience*, Vol. 6, No. 7: 669–673

Wilson, G., MacDonald, R., Byrne, C., Ewing, S. and Sheridan, M. (2008) 'Dread and Passion: Primary and Secondary Teachers' Views on Teaching the Arts', *Curriculum Journal*, Vol. 19, No. 1: 37–53

Young, S. (2003) *Music with the Under-Fours.* London: RoutledgeFalmer

Zhang, J., Harbottle, G., Wang, C. and Kong, Z. (1999) 'Oldest Playable Musical Instruments Found at Jiahu Early Neolithic Site in China', *Nature*, Vol. 401: 366–368

Zimmerman, F., Christakis, D. and Meltzoff, A. (2007) 'Associations between Media Viewing and Language Development in Children under Age 2 Years', *Journal of Pediatrics*, Vol. 151, No. 4: 334–336

4 Developing Imagination and Imaginative Play

Introduction

The value of play in supporting development has been a recurring theme in child development over many centuries. Rousseau, whose influence on early education was profound, wrote in his book *Emile* (Rousseau, 1911) that children should be allowed to develop free from the constraints of society. The idea of play was central to the development of early kindergartens (Froebel, 1826) as were the use of simple educational toys (called gifts by Froebel). Some of these toys, such as bricks, could be used in a variety of ways, stimulating imagination and this is a theme developed by Steiner's educational methods (see Steiner, 1996), where natural objects can be used creatively by children in their play, where dolls are genderless and faceless, to stimulate imagination and children are allowed the satisfaction of experiencing and learning through self-directed play (Oldfield, 2001). Piaget (1976) and Vygotsky (1962) identified the importance of different types of play for children's development, while in Maslow's (1968) hierarchy self-actualization involves an element if playfulness.

In the 1960s, the Plowden Report (DES, 1967) emphasized play and discovery learning and the importance of curiosity and imagination and led almost directly to the Early Years Foundation Stage (DCSF, 2008), via a number of different incarnations. In the Early Years Foundation Stage (DCSF, 2008) and other stages of learning (DfEE, 1999), play, imagination and creativity are actively encouraged. Other educational initiatives and educational writers advocate play (Lindon, 2001; Moyles, 2005; Johnston and Nahmad-Williams, 2008; Bruce, 2009) and imagination (Beetlestone, 1998; Duffy, 1998; Craft, 2000; DfES, 2003; Wilson, 2005) as essential ingredients to help achieve a variety of early developmental aims.

There are a number of different types of play and each can support different developmental aims. Solitary play, where children play alone, can be an early type of play, although it is also a feature of play in older children. A further development of solitary play is parallel play, termed companionship play by Bruce (2009), or playing alongside another child, with little or no communication, cooperation or collaboration. Cooperative/collaborative play involves children playing and interacting and can help children to develop understanding of how to play games with rules and understand social rules for effective interaction, as well as how to negotiate rules (see Johnston Nahmad-Williams, 2009). Piaget (1976) identified symbolic play in children between the ages of 2 and 6 years of age, when they acquire knowledge and understanding of the world around them and ludic play; play concerned with fantasy and role-play. It could be considered that over-reliance on epistemic play would provide children with skills but not the ability to transfer those skills to other contexts. Hutt et al., (1988) developed the definitions of both ludic play and epistemic play which develops knowledge and skills through problem solving and identified the problems of over-reliance on one type of play for balanced development (as will be discussed later in this chapter). Other types of play include socio-dramatic play where social interactions and personal and social issues can be re-enacted and exploratory play, where children use their senses to explore the world around them (see Johnston, 2005) and imaginative play where children use their imaginations in their play.

What is imagination and imaginative play?

Imagination is the innate ability to perceive an image or situation in the mind, rather than in the concrete. Through imagination, children make sense of the world and meaning to experience (Sutton-Smith, 1988) and can be expressed through imaginary friends, stories or fantasies. A psychological hypothesis for the development of human imagination is that it increases mental stimulation and helps to develop problem-solving abilities, although its relationship with creativity is well recognized (Beetlestone, 1998; Duffy, 1998; DfES, 2003). As a result, it is strange that in the Early Years Foundation Stage (DCSF, 2008) it is separated from creativity in the strands of development within the key area of Creative Development.

Like creativity, imagination is not a skill to be developed in the 'right' conditions or taught, but an innate ability, present in everyone and should be encouraged and supported. In young children imagination can take a number of forms such as,

1 Stories and games that mix fact and fiction – a form of blended learning (see Johnston, 2005). For example, many picture books contain factual information in either a fictional context, as in *The Hungry Caterpillar* (Carle, 1970) or use imagination to picture other contexts, as in *Where the Forest Meets the Sea* (Baker, 1987).
2 Imaginary people or friends – more common in firstborns and only children. These imaginary friends enable children to explore and express emotions and concerns, especially in situations where they feel they have little or no control. They also provide children opportunities for some degree of independence and secrecy.
3 Imagining scenes and situations in the mind while listening to stories or in role-play situations.
4 Using objects in imaginary ways during play.

In this way the types of play that are formed from the imagination are ludic play (fantasy and role-play), socio-dramatic (encompassing imaginary social interactions to solve personal and emotional problems) and imaginative play (using imagination in play).

Case study

Ashley, Brendan and Poppy were playing in the garden when Ashley noticed a large cardboard box, in which her parents' washing machine had been delivered. She turned it into a house in her game, using the open end as a door and drawing windows with a large marker pen on the side. Brendan and Poppy came to play with her and Ashley said 'Children, you are very naughty, you have got all muddy in the garden. You must wipe your feet before you come in the house' Poppy took off her shoes and got into the 'house' with Ashley. After a while, Poppy said, 'This is the house in the "Three Little Pigs"' and Brendan who was playing outside the 'house' said, 'I am the wolf, I am the wolf'. The three children then re-enacted the story of the *Three Little Pigs*, using the box as each house in turn. Brendan played the part of the wolf, but then became a pig when there was a need for a third pig.

Reflection for the early career professional

- What types of imaginative play were the children involved in at different parts of their play?
- How could an adult further encourage their imaginative play?
- How could you encourage more imaginative play with the children in your care?

Reflection for the leader/manager

- How does the organization of your setting support imaginative play?
- How do your colleagues currently use imaginative play to support child development?
- How could you promote different types of imaginative play in your setting?

Imagination is a well-recognized feature of creativity and adds to the quality of life as the following quotations show,

Imagination is the highest kite one can fly.

Lauren Bacall, actress (1924)

Imagination is more important than knowledge. For while knowledge defines all we currently know and understand, imagination points to all we might yet discover and create.

Albert Einstein, physicist (1879–1955)

To invent, you need a good imagination and a pile of junk.

Thomas A. Edison, inventor (1847–1931)

You cannot depend on your eyes when your imagination is out of focus.

Mark Twain, novelist, from
A Connecticut Yankee in King Arthur's Court (1835–1910)

Photograph 4.1 Children playing (© P. Hopkins)

Developing imagination and imaginative play from birth to 3 years of age

The beginning of imaginative play involves babies in enjoying patterns, colours, shapes, shadows and sounds and connecting them with pleasure. They learn to shake rattles or toys stretched across their prams, watch the movement of mobiles placed above their cots. They listen to songs and rhymes and make noises in response (Baby World 2009: webpage). While its difficult to see imagination in babies, we can see curiosity as when 'they find their hands and can't stop admiring them' and it is this that helps to develop imagination. Duffy (2004) also see curiosity as the beginnings of imagination, with imaginative children exploring and questioning. We can see imagination in a baby who when used to his father arriving home at bath-time, constantly looks towards the bathroom door waiting for him to come. Very young children will also imitate facial expressions, sounds and movements and so make connections with emotions and the beginnings of imagination (Abbot and Langston, 2005).

When children are able to move, their imagination is more evident in the way they play with toys and objects. Jamie, a 15-month-old child in a private nursery was introduced to an electrical hen that moved across the floor to the music and words of the *Birdie Song* (Tweets, 1981). While the music played, Jamie danced by wiggling his bottom and waving his arms and because his balance was not good, he often fell onto his bottom, but immediately got back up and started again. When the hen stopped moving, Jamie picked it up and took it to his carer to start it again. Throughout the whole 'performance', Jamie did not smile or giggle and took his dance very seriously, although he clearly enjoyed the music and dancing.

Children under 3 years of age will also use objects in an imaginary way, especially when they are the same shape, size or colour as the object they are pretending it to be. In this way a wooden block can be a mobile phone, a radio or a cake; a teddy bear can be a baby, a dog or a friend; a laundry basket can be a boat, a house or a car. In many ways, if we provide children with toys for every occasion, we are limiting their imagination.

Case study

Southgate Nursery created a small, fenced garden area for the children with a big tree, grass and flowerbed. The nursery manager asked the staff and parents how they thought they could develop it for the children. One suggestion was to permanently theme the area into a jungle with painting on the fence and jungle-themed climbing apparatus.

Reflection for the early career professional

- How do you think a permanent themed area would promote or limit imaginative play?
- How could you promote imaginative play in your own practice?

> **Case study—Cont'd**
>
> **Reflection for the leader/manager**
>
> Consider with your staff the merits of a permanent or no-permanent themed area for the promotion of imaginative play.
>
> - Why is one type of area better for imaginative play?
> - How could you develop your own play areas to promote different types of play, particularly imaginative play?

Developing imagination and imaginative play from 3 to 5 years of age

Three years of age is considered to be an important milestone in the development of imagination (Baby World, 2009), although this may be because imaginative play is more obvious and explicit at this age. Certainly, fact and fiction, myth and reality can become confused for children from 3 to 5 years of age. I have witnessed children looking at worms with magnifying glasses and imagining that it is a large snake, or listen to natural sounds in the environment and saying they can hear a lion roar (Johnston, 2005). They will also tell you a fictional story as an excuse for a misdemeanour and it does seem that they really believe the story they have created.

At this age, children will continue to imitate adults and other role models in their imaginative play and this can help their social, emotional and language development (see especially Book 1 of this series, *Personal, Social and Emotional Development*). When new babies join the family, children will play doctors and midwives and health visitors and care for their dolls as if they were babies. If they are feeling uncertain of their place in the family because of a new sibling, this may be reflected in their play and can identify when positive support is needed to help with feelings of jealousy or frustration. When they are struggling to share and cooperate with others in social situations, they may play a game with strict rules which will help them to understand the concepts of fairness, turn-taking and rules. These imitating play scenarios will enable a child to use the ideas or behaviours in other contexts.

Children between the ages of 3 and 5 will also create their play scenarios using available resources and, like the younger children, they will use the available resources imaginatively. An old sheet over a washing line or a clothes-horse can become a tent, a wigwam or a house. Leaves can act as plates, money, decorations or letters. As a young child, I would spend hours with a twig, making a family out of flower heads and parts of plants; faces were pansies, mother's dress was a hollyhock flower, father's trousers were lupin seeds etc. Even a pile of stones can be used to create patterns or structures. I do believe that in our desire to provide a wealth of play resources for children, we can limit their imagination. Sometimes a hat can be the only resource needed to enable imaginative play, being symbolic of a particular role; a builder's hard hat, a police helmet, a chef's hat, a Victorian bonnet etc. In creating a role-play area, children can play a major part in designing the area and deciding what resources should be collected and made. As they play in the role-play area, they will add to the resources to augment their play further.

Photograph 4.2 Child in role-play (Tracy Gannon)

Sometimes a story-book, story sack or nursery rhyme can stimulate imaginative play that starts with the story and develops in different directions. The story of Noah's ark can lead to a play with one particular family of animals, the rhyme *One, two, three four, five, once I caught a fish alive* can lead to an imaginary camping and fishing trip and the story-book *Home Before Dark* (Beck, 1997) can lead to re-enacting other fears and concerns that children may have. Puppets can help imaginative play by enabling children to explore tensions, emotions and behaviours and particularly support children who engage in solitary play and help the transition to more social play.

At 3 years of age, children are more likely to be solitary or play alongside other children, while as they get older, they will cooperate and collaborate in the play of others. Adults can support this transition from solitary to cooperative play by modelling play behaviours while playing with children. As they play together, children can be stimulated by the imaginations of others and take the play to new levels and dimensions and this will benefit other creative aspects of their development (dance, painting, language, design). For example, in a building site, role-play children can design and create structures, in imaginative play with musical instruments, children can compose music, or in imagining a Hindu wedding, children can dress in their best saris, decorate their hands with patterns and dance. In many ways the opportunities are limitless and the play can provide a link between their reality, the reality of others, legend/history, myth and fantasy.

Case study

The role-play area in a reception classroom was set up as a house with all the usual resources, such as cooking utensils, cutlery, plates, dolls, table and chairs. Josh, Kareene and Stephen were piling all the pots, pans and cutlery into the middle of the table. They were creating the TARDIS from Dr Who and the pile on the table was the central control panel. Josh put a pan on his head and repeated 'I am a Dalek' and 'Exterminate' in a robotic voice. Stephen was cupping his hands over his mouth and making different 'monster' sounds. Kareene was being The Doctor working the controls.

Reflection for the early career professional

Television programmes can often be the stimulus for imaginative play and you will often see children taking on the role of some of the characters.

- What are your views on the impact of popular culture on children's play?
- How might you resource the role-play area so that a range of different types of role-play can be supported?

Reflection for the leader/manager

- Discuss the impact of popular culture on children's play with your staff and find out their views. The chapter 'Teletubby Tales: Popular Culture and Media Education' (Marsh and Hallet, 1999: 153–174) would be useful to read to provide further information. How could your setting harness children's interests when motivated by popular culture?
- Consider boys' imaginative play in the role-play area. What appears to motivate them?

Transition to Key Stage 1 (5 to 7 years of age)

The transition in play from the EYFS (DCSF, 2008) to Key Stage 1 (DfEE, 1999) is possibly one of the most difficult. Children will often move from child-centred play contexts where they learn and develop through play, making decisions about how and what they learn to adult-initiated, curriculum-focused practical activities, which Bruce (2009) believes is not play. There is an interesting debate as to whether play should look and be different in educational settings (Moyles, 1989) or just have a different emphasis and maybe with different roles for practitioners (Johnston and Nahmad-Williams, 2008). Johnston and Nahmad-Williams (2008: 271) identify a dichotomy for Key Stage 1 teachers as 'if play is too directed it is deemed not to be play, yet there is a clear directive and need for play to be planned as part of the educational curriculum' and conclude that there is a 'need for a clear rationale for play in school'.

It is important to note that play does not stop at age 5 or when children start formal education. Remember too that in many countries formal education does not start until later than in the United Kingdom and a longer play-based curriculum appears to pay dividends in many areas of development and learning (OfSTED, 2003; UNICEF, 2007). Indeed, as adults we still learn through play and much of that play involves imagination. We play at computer games, imagine fictional lives when we read a book, watch a film or soap opera, or listen to radio plays and rehearse for job interviews and difficult situations. Some adults are involved in amateur dramatics or historical re-enactments or create imaginary worlds through painting, embroidery, poems and stories. Helen Bromley has had particular success in bringing play back into the curriculum for children of primary age, through small world play (Bromley, 2004a), imaginary use of everyday objects (Bromley, 2004b) and play boxes (Bromley, 2009) and the positive effects on learning are evident. Some schools include role-play areas in each class throughout the primary school in an attempt to raise standards, develop the children socially, emotionally as well as cognitively and motivate children to want to continue to learn.

Case study

The Year 1 children were doing a topic on 'How we used to live'. They had visited the museum and taken part in a Victorian washday. They had investigated the local area and identified Victorian houses. There was also a planned 'Victorian Day' in the school when staff and children would dress up and play Victorian games and take part in different activities. The class had turned their role-play area into a Victorian home. It had a cooking range, oil lamps, Victorian clothes, a dolly tub, dolly peg and wash board. The children had also painted the outside to match the brickwork seen on their walk in the local area. The children playing in the area kept to the Victorian theme most of the time. Occasionally children played in there as though it were a modern home. Girls were more interested in playing in the role-play area than boys.

Reflection for the early career professional

- How might the creation of the role-play area enhance children's understanding of the topic?

- Consider the advantages and disadvantages of having a role-play area with a very specific theme.

Reflection for the leader/manager

- Consider the provision for play for children in KS1. How might you enhance this provision?
- If you don't already have a policy for play in KS1, consider introducing one which takes account of children's physical, intellectual, social and emotional needs.

The role of imagination and imaginative play in child development

Imagination and imaginative play can support development and learning in a number of different areas. Reading can be encouraged by early books that provide visual, tactile and auditory stimulation, so babies are 'absorbed by the shiny pictures, crinkly material and buttons that make sounds' (Baby World, 2009: webpage). Older children can choose books and enjoy using their imagination while the story is being told (orally, with a book or by listening to stories on CDs) and in acting out the stories. All this will help motivate children to want to read and develop their listening skills and by recounting or acting out stories, their speaking skills.

As children act out stories or play in role-play areas, they love to dress up and the very act of dressing-up can help their fine motor coordination and physical skills. Dressing-up clothes are best if they are not too themed and specific, so that a shawl can be a headdress, a veil, a scarf, a blanket, a sari as well as a shawl. I was given some lovely dressing-up costumes by a dance school which was having a clear-out and while they were a wonderful resource, they were not as supportive of creativity and imagination as an old dress or a t-shirt. Creativity and imagination can be further developed through drawing and modelling creative ideas and by children making up their own small world play boxes or story sacks. Depending on the objects in the small world boxes, the children can be developing knowledge and understanding of the world.

I have shown boxes with a variety of small objects/toys to enable children to create dramas and play scenarios. In one box, I have out some leaves, twigs, stones, moss, straw, bark and a collection of plastic minibeasts; in another I have a collection of farm animals; in another some animal finger puppets. Using finger, shadow or glove puppets to re-create stories or act out imaginary or real events can support language, creative, physical and social development. Puppets can encourage children to create their own stories, to imagine characters and personalities and voices.

Free play

Free play can take a variety of forms (see Johnston and Nahmad-Williams, 2008) from total free play where the child initiates the play, sets it up and chooses resources, through to free play after set work has been completed. In between these extremes of free play are situations where a selection of resources are chosen by the professional and with the child able to move between activities, play situations set up by a professional and with the child making decisions about how to use the resources and play situations set up by the professional and with the children in groups, moving to new activities when told.

True free play is characterized by the children's freedom to control the play, make decisions about what they want to do and the time for children to fully immerse themselves in their play. Children do not want to be told what to play with, who to play with and how long to play as this restricts and devalues play and will produce fewer learning outcomes. If children are only allowed to play when they have finished directed tasks (seen as work by children, who consider work to be hard, unpleasant activity) some children will never get the chance to play and others will not fulfil the directed task to their best ability in the rush to get to the play activity. Free-flow play (Bruce, 2009) is play that provides the time and space for full involvement and enables children to move freely between play activities. In order for free-flow play to work, children do need to have some rules, such as how many children are allowed in any one area, some safety aspects and use of resources, although these should not restrict the quality of the involvement in the play.

Case study

Early Childhood Studies students at Bishop Grosseteste University College set up three play days, one for children in the Early Years Foundation Stage, one for children at Key Stage 1 and one for children at Key Stage 2. Each day used the same play areas and play resources (see Table 4.1) and while the students had to consider how the play area might need to be slightly different for different stages, the children provided the differentiation for themselves by playing differently. Children were also expected to move freely between play activities.

Table 4.1 Play Areas for EYFS, KS1 and KS2 Play

Area	Objectives	Resources
1. Garden Centre	**Communication, Language and Literacy:** Eric Carle 'The Tiny Seed' Writing labels for plants Vocabulary (e.g. plant, seed, soil, grow, root, shoot, leaf, flower)	Book by Eric Carle (1987) *The Tiny Seed* Collection of Seeds, seed packets, plants and flowers Plastic lolly stick labels (some blank and some with vocabulary on)
	Mathematical Development: Counting, sorting and buying/selling seeds and plants Knowledge and Understanding of the World: Parts of plants, variety of seeds and plants, growth of plants	Laminated white labels Dry-wipe pens Sorting hoops Shop front Till and money Trowel, wheelbarrow, rake etc. Compost and pots
	Personal, Social and Emotional Development: Social interaction, taking turns Care for living things Awareness of the needs of others including plants	
2. Travel Agent	**Communication, Language and Literacy:** Reading holiday brochures Passport Communicating with others Knowledge and Understanding of the World: ICT picture for passport using digital camera Places in the world Packing Teddy's bags	Holiday brochures Passport templates Laptop computer and printer Digital camera Teddy Suitcase Clothes etc.
	Personal, Social and Emotional Development: Social interaction	

⇨

Case study—Cont'd

Table 4.1 Cont'd

Area	Objectives	Resources
3. Building Site	**Communication, Language and Literacy:** Communication Vocabulary (describing materials in their own words, introduction of new words where appropriate, e.g. sand, brick, build, stable, safe, climb) **Mathematical Development:** Counting and sorting building materials **Physical Development** Building structures Climbing and balancing **Personal, Social and Emotional Development:** Social interaction, taking turns	Large bricks, blocks etc. Small building materials PE mats 2 A frames beam
4. Seaside	**Communication, Language and Literacy:** Seaside books Vocabulary (shell, fish, swim, sand, sea etc.) Writing postcards home **Mathematical Development:** Sorting seaside objects Knowledge and Understanding of the World: Variety of life in and around the seaside Materials and their properties – sand and water play **Creative development** Printing with fish and seaside objects Shell pictures	Story and information books Collection of seaside objects Sorting hoops Brine shrimps Sand, water trays and play equipment Flat fish, whole prawns Shells, sponges and other seaside objects for printing Printing inks, trays and sponges Pasta shells (different colours) paper and glue
5. Space Rocket	**Communication, Language and Literacy:** Space books Language for communication **Physical Development:** Dressing up Crawling **Creative development** Making space rocket with junk material	Space Rocket with computer console, telephones, levers etc. Tunnel Astronauts' and aliens' clothes Junk material Paint, brushes, glue etc.

⇨

Concerns expressed by students and professionals (particularly those at Key Stage 2) included:

- How to attract children to an activity if they had free-choice;
- How children will learn if they are allowed to play and not directly 'taught';
- How children will move freely between activities and abide by the rules themselves (no more than 6 in any play area, be safe, respect each other);
- How the play can be suitable for children at different ages.

The resulting play was very purposeful and successful in achieving the learning objectives appropriate for their age. The students were very surprised when on the first day children arrived and two 3-year-old girls ignored the exciting play activities and sat on a bean bag drawing for about 30 minutes. They and the professionals were also very pleased that children motivated themselves, organized themselves and used the resources in different ways to those planned. For example, one child playing in a role-play area set up as a building site, took some green material and wrapping himself up became first a 'caterpillar', then a 'cocoon' and finally taking some orange material became a 'butterfly' (Johnston, 2009).

Practical task

Set up your own imaginative play area with opportunities for free play and collect evidence on the learning and development that occurs.

Reflection for the early career professional

- How effective was the play in developing the learning objectives you had set?
- How did the play address concerns you had about free play?
- How might you organize imaginative play in the future?

Reflection for the leader/manager

- How effective did you and your staff feel the play was for different ages and children in your setting?
- How did the play address concerns your staff had about free play?
- How might you organize imaginative play in the future to effectively include more children, develop more objectives and especially develop imagination?

Structured play

Structured play can be considered a misnomer and be unhelpful to professionals (Moyles, 1989) as it implies that it is only structured play that has adult support and scaffolding of learning (Vygotsky, 1962) and the teacher learning alongside the learner (Stone, 1993), when clearly no play activities are devoid of any adult support. Structured play, like unstructured play can also take a variety of forms. It can involve professionals selecting resources and children choosing from the selection and moving freely between the activities. It can involve children being given a specific task to complete with the resources, such as make an animal with the playdough or design a hat for Teddy. It can be led by the professional and have a specific outcome, pre-decided by the professional. The first two types of structured play do provide opportunities for the use of imagination, but the last type has very limited opportunities for use of the imagination, even if the professional has used theirs in planning the activity. Perhaps in looking at play led fully by the professional the idea of 'shared control', based on the High/Scope philosophy (see Holt, 2007), is more appropriate. What seems to be important is that the professional respects the child's interests and there are opportunities for the child to decide the direction of play and that there is an effective relationship between the child and professional, so that children feel able to take the play into new directions and make choices for themselves.

Case study

The teacher read *Where the Wild Things Are* (Sendak, 1963) to her class supported by a story sack, which included the characters of Max and the Wild Things, a blue piece of shiny material for the sea, a boat, cardboard scenery depicting the forest and another depicting Max's bedroom. After the story, the teacher put the story sack on the carpet, removed the boat, and asked the children to find a way for Max to cross the water back home because his boat had gone missing. The teacher noticed that although the children were happy to play with the characters, none were actually trying to solve the problem of Max crossing the water back home. She decided to join the play and asked how Max might get home. One child said 'He can fly' and proceeded to 'fly' Max over the water and put him in his bedroom.

The teacher didn't say anything but went to get the Lego and started to fix pieces together. She then said she was trying to make a plane but couldn't work out how to put the wings on. One child said he was going to make a rocket and two other children started to help him. Another child said he was going to make a helicopter. None of them referred to the story or the character of Max but were very interested in making their models.

Reflection for the early career professional

- Why do you think the children were not interested in solving the problem that the teacher had set for them?
- What strategies did the teacher use to try and involve the children in solving the problem?
- How would you have used the story sack and why?

Reflection for the leader/manager

- Discuss the term 'structured play' with your staff to see if you all have a shared understanding.
- How does structured play in your setting follow the philosophy of shared control?
- Encourage staff to share examples of where a structured play situation has been directed by the child/children, which has enhanced the learning experience.

One way of structuring play is to allow children time to freely explore resources before structuring an activity and then to allow further free play, initiated by the children, which may well be enhanced by the period of structured play (Moyles, 1989). This enables children to build on their experiences, benefit from a scaffolded activity, but still be given the freedom to develop the play in the direction they wish to follow. Adults need to be sensitive to the children's play and be willing to stand back and observe. Bruce (2004) refers to inner and outer play: inner play being through the brain and the child's own motivations and outer play being based on the influences of the people with whom the child interacts. It is useful to observe the children at play and note the instances of inner and outer play and how it impacts upon the play situation (see Broadhead et al., 2010).

Outdoor play

Outdoor play provides a wealth of opportunities for imaginative play. High quality outdoor play is recognized as an important part of the Early Years Foundation Stage (Doherty and Bailey, 2003; DCSF, 2008). Bilton (1998) and Bruce (2009) agree on the advantages of less division between the outdoor and indoor play areas so that free play involves the children in feely moving from one play area to the other. The possibilities of this are limited by the staffing in the setting, the size of the areas and setting itself. However, where settings allow greater autonomy and freedom and trust, the children do appear to benefit and do not need as close supervision as when directed. Increased levels of supervision because of health and safety issues have not only had a negative impact on freedom and independence in outdoor play, but also on the opportunities for imagination. In Johnston and Nahmad-Williams (2008: 274), we identify that 'a rain shower can cause mayhem with the rush to get inside

Photograph 4.3 Playing outside (© Emma Jordan)

as though it were acid, not rainwater! Yet children love splashing in puddles and learn so much about their environment through seeing and experiencing the changes'. A rain shower also provides opportunities for imaginative play, by imagining the rain on your face in a warmer climate, the world in a puddle or the effect of the rain on minibeasts and plants. A puddle can become a sea or lake for a boat (maybe with a twig acting as a boat) or a swimming pool or beach for small world play. Wet soil can be used to make imaginary houses, roads and mountains, with leaves, twigs and stones as other resources.

Case study

The reception class in a village primary school has a small quadrangle outside the classroom with hard paving and concrete pillars. This can be accessed from a glass door in the classroom. The quadrangle leads directly onto the large playground which has gates leading out onto the street. There is a large field but that is on the other side of the playground at the furthest distance from the reception classroom. The sand and water trays are put outside the glass door in good weather that the children can access freely. The teacher takes the whole class outside once a week to play with the wheeled toys on the playground. In summer, the teacher takes the whole class out to play on the field about once every two weeks. She sets this up at lunchtime taking out boxes of books, bats and balls, large construction toys and dressing-up clothes. OfSTED have stated in their report on the school that children should have more access to outdoor play.

Reflection for the early career professional

- If you were this teacher, how would you provide more access to outdoor play?
- What sort of experiences are children missing out on in the current system that is in place? How could you provide these experiences?

Reflection for the leader/manager

- If you were able to secure some funding, what changes would you make to the outdoor environment?
- If this were your school and you could not change the access to the outdoors, what systems and strategies would you put in place to ensure the children experienced a full range of outdoor play opportunities?

There is a wide range of equipment that can be purchased to resource an outdoor area. Some of this is fixed equipment such as climbing frames and swings and although these costly items look impressive and do have benefits, they also have their limitations (Johnston and Nahmad-Williams, 2009). Smaller apparatus and more flexible equipment that can be moved can provide similar benefits but have the advantage of being less costly and more adaptable. The natural environment can be manipulated to create small mounds, slopes and concave areas to play on and in, and logs, willow and imaginative planting can provide seating, dens and enclosed areas. As well as visiting other outdoor play areas, to gather ideas for the development of your own area it is a good idea to visit woods and gardens to stimulate the imagination to create an outdoor area that provides children with the opportunity to play and interact with their natural environment.

Drama in the EYFS and Key Stage 1

Young children's play leads effortlessly into drama. Their capacity for imaginative play, exploring characters and narratives, and their inherent inclination to pretend and engage in role-play means that drama is a natural extension of that which is already spontaneous in the child. Through drama we are harnessing children's play by providing the content and the contexts (Toye and Prendiville, 2000). It is important to make the distinction between drama and theatre. Theatre is a specific discipline which takes account of communicating with the audience and skills in stagecraft. This is not what we are advocating. Drama is about process and does not need to culminate in any sort of production or performance. Lambirth (2005: 86) defines this as 'process drama' which is 'not audience-centred but child-centred'. It does not need a professional who is an actor to support the children. The main skill an early-years professional needs is the capacity to pretend and to know the purpose of the drama in terms of children's development.

Story is a natural stimulus for drama. One of the most common ways to use drama and story is by asking the children to re-enact the story. This may show that the children have followed the narrative but does not develop understanding or imagination. Children may well retell the story in their imaginary play, but drama should extend the experience by focusing on specific characters, key moments in the plot or by exploring aspects of the story that are not part of the main narrative. If the professional directs the retelling 'the children become mere puppets in the process' (Toye and Prendiville, 2000: 17). For example, in *Owl Babies* (Waddell, 1994), the focus could be on the three baby owls and how they are feeling when their mother is gone and they don't know where she is. The practitioner could focus on one of the illustrations and ask a child to be Sarah (oldest baby owl) and ask how she is feeling, what she thinks about her brothers or what she would do if her mother isn't home by morning. We know the mother is gone and that she comes back but we don't know what she did while she was away. The children could be supported in creating 'Mummy's Story' by drawing a story map of her journey and acting out specific parts such as when she nearly got caught by a fox or when she flew into the wrong nest. There could also be a focus on events before a story starts or after it has ended. For example, why did Goldilocks go in and wreck the Three Bears' House? Why was she in the woods? What did her mum and dad do when they realized she was missing? When Goldilocks got home, what did she say to the policeman her mum and dad had called? The way the drama is organized is up to the professional. It could be through hotseating where a child or adult takes on the role of the character and answers questions or if it is based on action, the whole group could mime an event. Two or three children could act out the scene and the professional could stop the action and ask the rest of the group to give advice.

Teacher in role

Teacher in role is an excellent tool to use with young children. This involves the adult taking on the role of a character and in this way the action can be guided by the professional. It is important that the children know when the professional is in a role and when they are being the teacher. This can be indicated by a visual aid such as wearing a scarf when in role or by some other signal. I just used to clap and say 'in role' or 'out of role' which the children fully understood. I used teacher in role with a reception class after reading *The Selfish Giant* (Wilde, 2001). I was in role as a very miserable old man who had a very big garden but who hated children because they kept playing in it and were noisy and broke the flowers. The children were the children in the story who lived in homes without gardens and wanted somewhere to play. The children had to persuade me, in role, to let them play. I did this with the whole class and occasionally came out of role to discuss things that had been said. Eventually the children persuaded me by agreeing to help me with the garden by planting vegetables and weeding. They would only play in one part of it and not when I was having my afternoon nap. Another example of teacher in role with the whole class was when we were all in a (imaginary) ship. We all had jobs to do, some were cooks, some were scrubbing the deck, some were steering the ship. I suddenly shouted that there was a leak and we proceeded to try and fix it. If the action was flagging I would call out something else, such as a fire in the kitchen or rocks ahead. In this way I was providing content and context but the children were in control of their own actions and interactions. Some were happy to just mime, others were more vocal and made suggestions and moved the drama forward.

One of the advantages of using teacher in role is the way the professional can guide the drama from within in a natural way. If the adult is outside the drama, it could be over-directed or left to flounder with children unsure of what to do. Children may also feel inhibited because they are aware that the adult is watching them and feel that they are being judged, which is moving the drama away from process drama because the teacher becomes the audience. Another advantage of teacher in role is the ability to be in the action and then step out to reflect on the action which further enhances the potential for the drama.

Practical tasks

Select a story that you know well. Consider events that might have happened before the story began with one or more of the characters. Consider the features of plot (events that change the action or move it forward) and consider the key features of the characters with particular focus on their emotions. Think of some possible scenarios for after the story has ended. Using one or more of your ideas, plan a drama session. Take account of how you will organize it, if you will use teacher in role and what you hope the children will learn from the experience.

Reflection for the early career professional

- Which parts of this process did you find easy and which were more difficult?
- If you were going to do this with children, what would be your main concerns and how might you overcome these?

Reflection for the leader/manager

- How much drama is planned for in your setting and what is its purpose?
- How might you support staff in developing their confidence in using drama with the children?
- Encourage your staff to use teacher in role and ask them to reflect on the experience.

Drama can stand alone as a process that helps to develop problem solving, dealing with feelings and emotions, confidence and self-esteem, negotiating skills, communication skills, understanding characters' actions, understanding the development of plot, and as an activity that is fun and engaging. It can also lead onto other outcomes. Referring to the scenarios already outlined, the children may write a letter to the Selfish Giant outlining the agreement; they might design the Giant's garden or they could plant vegetables. The children could write an account of the disaster at sea for a newspaper or experiment in the water tray with how to keep a boat afloat that has a hole in it. Goldilocks could send a card saying sorry to the Three Bears. The children could find out which other animals are nocturnal to make a list of who the Owl Mother might have met on her journey. Drama can be linked to all areas of the curriculum and is an excellent way of developing understanding in an active and stimulating way. Sometimes drama can be a spontaneous event but it is usually most successful when it is planned for with a clear objective, specific context, clear organization and roles. However, flexibility is important (Cremin, 2007) so that the children have shared control and are partners in directing and guiding the drama. It is also vital that clear ground rules are set so that children know when to stop and know when the teacher is in or out of role.

Movement and mime

One very effective way of developing children's imagination is through movement and mime. There are a number of published schemes that provide music and stories for movement but an imaginative practitioner can provide stimuli and support that can be personalized for a particular group of children or topic. There are a number of ideas that could be developed such as a toyshop coming to life with children being rag dolls, robots, Jack-in the boxes, trainsets, dinosaurs; a jungle with lions, snakes, monkeys, spiders; a factory with machines that go up and down, in and out, turn round, slow down, speed up; a circus with tumbling clowns, acrobats, horses, tightrope walkers; a city with traffic in a traffic jam or coming across traffic lights, people rushing, answering mobile phones, putting up umbrellas, waiting a queue, trying to cross a road, waving at someone they know across the street – the possibilities are endless. Music can be used to support the movement and mime such as excerpts from CDs or can be created using percussion instruments or the voice. Published stories such as 'We're Going on a Bear Hunt' (Rosen and Oxenbury, 2001) are very useful to use for movement or stories can be created by the practitioner. Stories which include travelling, exploring, or allow the children to display a range of emotions are particularly effective.

Case study

The teacher was telling the story in the hall and the children were acting it out through mime and movement:

> You are walking down the street feeling happy. You start to skip and then you have to stop to cross the road. Look right, then left, then right again and – oh – stop a car is coming. Look again – it's safe to cross so off you go. You have to open a large gate to enter a wood. It's very heavy. You have to really push – push harder! It's open now so in you go. Watch out for those branches – push them out of the way. You will have to climb over the log and be careful over those stepping stones over the stream. That's it – you're over. Oh it's a bit muddy. Your feet are getting stuck in the thick mud. That's it – pull them out. You are on lovely soft grass now, walking happily on the grass. You can see the sea! Run towards the sea! You're on the sand now – it's a bit soft – so you can't move too quickly. You're at the water's edge now – take off your shoes and socks. Paddle in the water. Oooh it's a bit cold! Watch out for the wave! Run out of the sea! Oh it's hard to run in water. Keep going – push your way through the water. You're back on the sand. You are feeling tired. You lie on the warm, soft sand. The sun is beating down on you and you close your eyes.

What's that? You can hear a noise? A snuffling noise. You sit up and look round. You are near a shed and the noise is coming from the shed. Walk to the shed to see if you can see in the window. Peer in. You can see something moving and can hear scrabbling and scratching. What is it? Now in a moment you are going to open the shed door and when I clap my hands I want you to become whatever it is that you can see in the shed. It's up to you – you decide what is in your shed. 1, 2, 3, (teacher claps her hands).

Reflection for the early career professional

- What skills are the children using during this activity?
- How might this activity promote children's imaginative skills?
- Consider creating your own story that includes both the children following your story and creating part of the story themselves
- How could this activity be developed?

Reflection for the leader/manager

- How do your staff use movement and story to promote imaginative skills?
- What types of resources could be put in place to support this?
- With your staff, generate a list of stories that would be effective to use with movement and mime.

References

Abbott, L. and Langston, A. (2005) 'Learning to Play: Babies and Young Children Birth to 3'. In Moyles, J. R. (ed.) *The Excellence of Play*. 2nd Edition. Buckingham: Open University Press, 27–38

Baby World, (2009) 'Baby Development – Imagination'. www.babyworld.co.uk/information/baby/baby_development/imagination.asp accessed 12/6/09

Baker, J. (1987) *Where the Forest Meets the Sea*. London: Walker Books

Beck, I. (1997) *Home Before Dark*. London: Scholastic

Beetlestone, F. (1998) *Creative Children, Imaginative Teaching*. Buckingham: Open University Press

Bilton, H. (1998) *Outdoor Play in the Early Years*. London: David Fulton

Broadhead, P., Johnston, J., Tobbell, C. and Woolley, R. (2010) *Personal, Social and Emotional Development*. London: Continuum

Bromley, H. (2004a) *The Small World Recipe Book 50 Exciting Ideas for Small World Play*. Birmingham: Lawrence Educational Publications

Bromley, H. (2004b) *Extraordinary Things to Do with Ordinary Objects*. Birmingham: Lawrence Educational Publications

Bromley, H. (2009) 'Story Boxes'. www.yellow-door.net/products/products_talk_for_writing_storyboxes.html

Bruce, T. (2004) *Developing Learning in Early Childhood*. London: Paul Chapman

Bruce, T. (2009) *Early Childhood*. 2nd Edition. London: Sage

Carle, E. (1970) *The Very Hungry Caterpillar*. Harmondsworth: Penguin

Carle, E. (1987) *The Tiny Seed*. London: Hodder and Stoughton

Craft, A. (2000) *Creativity Across the Primary Curriculum*. London: Routledge

Cremin, T. (2007) 'Drama'. In Cremin, T. and Dombey, H. (eds) *Handbook of Primary English in Initial Teacher Education*. Cambridge: NATE/UKLA, 115–128

DCSF (2008) *The Early Years Foundation Stage; Setting the Standard for Learning, Development and Care for Children from Birth to Five; Practice Guidance*. London: DCSF

DES (1967) *Children and Their Primary School. A Report of the Central Advisory Council for Education (England) Vol. 1: Report*. London: HMSO

DfEE (1999) *The National Curriculum: Handbook for Teachers in England*. London: DfEE/QCA

DfES (2003) *Excellence and Enjoyment. A Strategy for Primary Schools*. London: DfES

Doherty, J. and Bailey, R. (2003) *Supporting Physical Development and Physical Education in the Early Years*. Buckingham: Open University Press

Duffy, B. (1998) *Supporting Creativity and Imagination in the Early Years*. Buckingham: Open University Press

Duffy, B. (2004) 'Creativity Matters'. In Abbott, L. and Langston, A. (eds) *Birth to Three Matters: Supporting the Framework of Effective Practice*. Maidenhead: Open University Press, 151–161

Froebel, F. (1826) *On the Education of Man*. Keilhau, Leipzig: Wienbrach

Holt, N. (2007) *Bringing the High/Scope Approach to Your Early Years Practice*. London: David Fulton

Hutt, C., Tyler, S., Hutt, J., and Christopherson, H. (eds) (1988) *Play, Exploration and Learning*. London: Routledge

Johnston, J. (2005) *Early Explorations in Science*. 2nd Edition. Maidenhead: Open University Press

Johnston, J. (2009) 'Science at Key Stage 1'. In Bruce, T. (ed) *Early Childhood*. 2nd Edition. London: Sage, 264–277

Johnston, J. and Nahmad-Williams, L. (2009) *Early Childhood Studies*. Harlow: Pearsons

Lambirth, A. (2005) *Primary English Reflective Reader*. Exeter: Learning Matters

Lindon, J. (2001) *Understanding Children's Play*. Cheltenham: Nelson Thornes

Maslow, A. H. (1968) *Towards a Psychology of Being*. New York: D. Van Nostrand Co

Marsh, J. and Hallet, E. (eds) (1999) *Desirable Literacies*. London: Paul Chapman Publishing Ltd

Moyles, J. (1989) *Just Playing?: The Role and Status of Play in Early Childhood Education*. Milton Keynes: Open University Press

Moyles, J. R. (ed.) (2005) *The Excellence of Play*. 2nd Edition. Buckingham: Open University Press

Ofsted (2003) *The Education of Six Year Olds in England, Denmark and Finland*. London: HMI

Oldfield, L. (2001) *Free to Learn. Introducing Steiner Waldorf Early Childhood Education*. Stroud, Gloucestershire: Hawthorn Press

Piaget, J. (1976) 'Mastery Play' and 'Symbolic Play'. In Bruner, J., Jolly, A. and Sylva, K. (eds) *Play – Its role in Development and Evolution.* Middlesex: Penguin, 166–171 and 555–569

Rosen, M. and Oxenbury, H. (2001) *We're Going on a Bear Hunt.* London: Walker Books Ltd

Rousseau, J. J. (1911) *Emile.* London : J. M. Dent and Sons

Sendak, M. (1963) *Where the Wild Things Are.* New York: HarperCollins

Steiner, R. (1996) *The Education of the Child and Early Lectures on Education.* New York: Anthroposophic Press

Stone, C. A. (1993) 'What is missing in the metaphor of scaffolding?'. In Forman, E. A., Minick, N. and Stone, C. A. (eds). *Contexts for Learning; Sociocultural Dynamics in Children's Development.* New York: Oxford University Press, 169–183

Sutton-Smith, Brian (1988) 'In Search of the Imagination'. In Egan, K. and Nadaner, D. (eds) *Imagination and Education.* New York: Teachers College Press, 3–29

Tweets (1981) *Birdie Song*

Toye, N. and Prendiville, F. (2000) *Drama and Traditional Story in the Early Years.* London: RoutledgeFalmer

UNICEF, (2007) *An Overview of Child Well-Being in Rich Countries. A Comprehensive Assessment of the Lives and Well-Being of Children and Adolescents in the Economically Advanced Nations.* Florence, Italy: Unicef

Vygotsky, L. (1962) *Thought and Language.* Cambridge, MA: MIT Press

Waddell, M. (1994) *Owl Babies.* London: Walker Books Ltd

Wilde, O. (2001) *The Selfish Giant.* London: Penguin Young Readers

Wilson, A. (2005) *Creativity in Primary Education.* London: Learning Matters

Conclusion

The series editors and authors hope that you find this book of interest and use to you in your professional work. If you would like to read more about the subject area, we recommend the following reading and websites to you.

Further reading

Dalcroze, J. (1967) *Rhythm, Music and Education*. Geneva: The Dalcroze Society

Goodkin, D. (2002) *Play, Sing and Dance: An Introduction to Orff Schulwerk*. New York: Schott

MacGregor, H. and Gargrave, B. (2001) *Let's Go Zudie-o*. London: A and C Black

MacGregor, H. and Gargrave, B. (2003) *Let's Go Shoolie-Shoo*. London: A and C Black

If you would like to read more about other key areas of the Early Years Foundation Stage, please see the following:

Beckley, P., Compton, A., Johnston, J. and Marland, H. (2010) *Problem Solving, Reasoning and Numeracy*. London: Continuum

Broadhead, P., Johnston, J., Tobbell, C. and Woolley, R. (2010) *Personal, Social and Emotional Development*. London: Continuum

Callander, N. and Nahmad-Williams, N. (2010) *Communication, Language and Literacy*. London: Continuum

Cooper, L. and Doherty, J. (2010) *Physical Development*. London: Continuum

Cooper, L., Johnston, J., Rotchell, E. and Woolley, R. (2010) *Knowledge and Understanding of the World*. London: Continuum

Useful websites

www.bongoclub.org.uk
  Bongo Club Youth Music – for parents and practitioners of 0–5 year olds
www.singup.org
  Sing up – the Music Manifesto's National Singing Programme
www.youthmusic.org.uk
  Youth music – research, resources, articles
www.dalcroze.org.uk

Dalcroze Eurhythmics method – developing understanding of music through movement

www.communitydance.org.uk

Foundation for Community Dance – making dance matter

www.ndta.org.uk

National Dance Teachers Association

www.tradamis.org

TRADAMIS – Traditional Music and Dance in Schools

Index